Black People
BREATHE

Zee Clarke

Black People
BREATHE

A Mindfulness Guide to Racial Healing

Illustration by Princella Seripenah

TEN SPEED PRESS
California | New York

Contents

To Dr. Harriett Jenkins (1926–2016) and
all the voices that continue to fight for change.

Introduction

Angry. Frustrated. Undervalued. Shocked. Sad. Attacked. Ashamed. Anxious. This is only a fraction of what Black people feel when we experience racism. Doctors and psychologists have discovered that the experience of racism can result in a wide range of health impacts that kill us slowly—death by a thousand cuts. Researchers at Columbia University found that racism causes traumatic stress, linked to negative mental-health outcomes such as depression, anger, hypervigilance, and low self-esteem. Chronically high levels of stress hormones in the bloodstream cause severe physical consequences, and racism has been linked to significantly higher rates of both heart disease and high blood pressure in African Americans. Studies also find that racial discrimination causes unhealthy behaviors, including overeating and substance abuse.

We can't wait for other people to get "woke," because we'll lose too many of our own people in the process. But there is something that we *can* do to begin healing. It's a "secret" that's been around for thousands of years. I discovered it when I was in Oakland, California, and then in India, where I explored it further. So, what is it?

Mindfulness.

It's the cheapest medical treatment you'll find on the market, and without a long list of side effects. Mindfulness doesn't require meditating in an ashram or a monastery. Something as simple as taking a deep breath qualifies as mindfulness, and it can literally change the way you feel physically, mentally, and emotionally.

I used to think that meditation and yoga were not for people who looked like me. The few times that I attended any such classes, I was the only Black person in the room, which only solidified this misconception.

However, the more I learned, the more I realized that Black people actually need these practices the most. And they work. Studies show that mindfulness practices reduce stress, blood pressure, heart disease, and so many more health issues that Black people face on a daily basis as a direct result of the harsh impact of systemic racism, microaggressions, and overt hate crimes on our lives. These practices can be used regardless of your religion, and you will feel the effects in real time.

In the following chapters, I'm going to share my personal experiences as a Black woman in America and the specific mindfulness and breathwork practices that have worked for me. Don't just take my word for it—the best way to truly understand and experience the benefits is to try them out. This isn't a book to read once and then let sit on your shelf. This is the ultimate guide to your mental and physical health when it comes to racism. The next time you're stopped by the police, the next time someone touches your hair without asking, the next time a white person says or does something that makes you so angry that you want to do something more Malcolm X than MLK, come back to this book for specific breathwork or mindfulness techniques that you can use to heal. Video tutorials of key practices can be found at zeeclarke.com/resources to guide you along the way.

It is our right to survive. It is our right to thrive. Mindfulness and breathwork will help you do just that.

Please Note

Although this book is written for Black people and tailored to the Black experience in America, those of other backgrounds who experience similar challenges can also benefit from the tools that I will share. To my white friends, I invite you to educate yourself about the Black experience, with an intention informed by both empathy and action. I also invite you to think about what role you might play to accelerate change.

**My mission in life is not merely to survive,
but to thrive.**

—Dr. Maya Angelou

CHAPTER ONE

Black People Breathe

I went to a violin vigil, not a protest. I didn't pack any tear-gas protection. I didn't pack any other recommended protest supplies. So, when I found myself clutching my violin, sprinting away from riot police amid a swarm of bodies all seeking safety from those that were supposed to protect us, I felt like I was in a dream, a dream that was not mine, a dream that I did not choose.

The plan was for violinists to meet in a park in Aurora, Colorado, to play together in honor of Elijah McClain. He played violin for the kittens in an animal shelter. The twenty-three-year-old Black man was sweet and kind, and was unarmed when he was killed by the Aurora police during his walk home from a convenience store. The same day as the violin vigil, there was also a peaceful march in honor of his life that ended where the violin vigil began. Dozens of musicians were playing their hearts out in sadness and solidarity when the riot police arrived. As the police advanced, protestors locked arms in a human chain around the violinists, trying to protect them from the officers. But what ended up happening was lots of chaos. We packed up our instruments and ran. It's all still very much a blur. I remember someone directing us toward a nearby place to regroup. I remember debating whether to get the hell out of there and just find my car immediately. However, something inside me knew I needed to stay. We found a place a quarter of a mile west and started to play once again, hoping the police wouldn't come our way.

"Say his name!" yelled Ashanti Floyd, "the Mad Violinist" and six-time-Grammy-nominated artist.

"Elijah McClain!" we chanted, with violins in hand and a demand for justice in our hearts.

"Say his name!" he repeated through the megaphone, while standing in the bed of a black pickup truck, the getaway vehicle in case the police decided to attack us again.

"Elijah McClain!" we chanted in unison, standing our ground. And to the sounds of police brutality and tear-gas canisters, to the sounds of helicopters above our heads, our violins sang songs of peace, songs of justice, songs of unity.

When I woke up the next morning, I was filled with rage. I was filled with sadness. I was also filled with the comfort of knowing that I wasn't alone. And yet pain in my heart and in my belly was screaming for attention. He was a Black violinist, and I was a Black violinist. He was a vegetarian, and I was a vegetarian. There aren't that many of us out there in this world. We, Black vegetarian violinists, could count one another on two hands. And, in this unicorn camaraderie, he was me and I was him. But I was still alive, and his last words continued to echo in my psyche.

The sound of his voice, pleading. The love in his heart, still present, while under attack. It was too much to process. Too much to handle. And I needed to breathe.

My heart rate skyrocketed and I felt overwhelmed in a swirl of despair. Why won't this stop? Why do white people hate us? Why can't we walk home from the grocery store without worrying about being harassed, and in this case, murdered, by the police? I'm tired of hearing "I can't breathe." Over and over again. I can't breathe. I can't breathe.

I.
CAN'T.
BREATHE.

Do they not hear us? Do they not care? Are we less worthy? Do they believe that we don't have the right to breathe? Why? *Why?* WHYYYYYYYY?

The thoughts wouldn't stop. The emotions overtook me like a massive wave, slamming me to the bottom of the ocean, blinded, flipped upside down, incapable of finding my own two feet, incapable of locating the ground. I completely lost my sense of control. I felt defeated.

And then, in my deepest moment of despair, I remembered a simple breathing technique that I had learned during my time in India—the Three-Part Breath for grounding. If you ever feel this overwhelmed and hopeless, I invite you to give it a try.

Inhale deeply, and feel the air enter your throat, fill your chest, and ultimately expand your belly like a balloon. As you exhale, feel your belly button move back toward your spine, as the air comes up through your chest, back through your throat, and out of your nostrils once again. As you inhale, you can say to yourself, "Throat . . . chest . . . belly," so that you can direct the breath appropriately. As you exhale, you can say, "Belly . . . chest . . . throat." Take three deep breaths like this and see how you feel.

When I did this during this emotionally charged moment, I felt my shoulders come down from around my ears. I felt my heart rate gradually slow. I felt like I was going to be okay—a sense of comfort. I was grateful that I knew what to do with myself in this state, because this hadn't always been the case. I used to get wrapped up in the swirl for hours, for days, sometimes weeks. The stories, the questions, the anger, would just play in my head on repeat and I would feel horrible.

I used to think that yoga, meditation, and "that white hippie stuff," as my Black friends called it, wasn't for me. Most of the marketing and media that I saw about these practices featured primarily white faces. In addition, these tools were never framed in a way that I could relate to. They seemed almost irrelevant to my life and my problems. However, mindfulness practices have been scientifically proven to reduce stress, manage heart issues and high blood pressure, improve sleep quality, and provide a sense of calm and inner peace. When applied to the specific challenges that Black people face, these practices can lead to incredible results.

For a long time, I thought to myself, *Black people don't have time for no meditation!* And then it happened. Did you ever play the game Mercy as a child, where you interlock fingers with a partner and squeeze and twist and turn until the pain just gets too much for the losing party, who screams "Mercy!" to make it end? That was my life. And that's how I ended up finally saying, I'll try anything, even the "white hippie stuff."

I had multiple friends die way too young. A friend once told me that friendship with me increases one's likelihood of an early death—and then he died also. Although some died from things like car accidents, my closest friends died from the substances that they abused to escape the pain of their lives. The pain of being Black and gay in America. The pain of trying to make ends meet when societal structures were already stacked against your whole family because of your race. The pain of having to pretend to be strong, because that is what Black people have to be. We have no choice.

Losing a loved one was a deep and painful experience. Losing multiple loved ones just deepened the pain and made it last longer. This grief was just the cherry on top of a life in which I constantly felt like the world was against me, like I needed to fight every day for what came so easily to others who didn't look like me. The cumulative racism in my lived experience, both at work and in my everyday life, was just too much. I screamed "Mercy!" and then I found mindfulness, breathwork, and so many other tools that have changed my life.

My friend Julian told me that he had started meditating and was seeing some tangible benefits in how he was feeling on a daily basis, in terms of both productivity and his ability to focus. "Really?" I said in disbelief. That's not for us. That's not what *we* do! But I trusted him, and I was open to trying anything. He said he was doing a mantra meditation. This is when you repeat a phrase over and over again and eventually fall into a meditative state. I tried it with some recordings and mantras I found online. They were in Sanskrit, and I could never remember the words. They were just too foreign to me. Even after I looked up the definitions, I still couldn't repeat them so that they really meant something to me. So, I gave up and said to myself again, "Meditation is not for me."

When my problems didn't go away, I decided to give it another shot. I attended an all-day retreat at the East Bay Meditation Center (EBMC) in Oakland, California, an introduction to meditation for beginners. EBMC is where I really learned to meditate. Having a community to learn with was so powerful. Having a queer woman of color as my teacher was even more powerful. This was not the typical blond woman I was used to seeing in the media, meditating on a beach. These were ordinary people who looked like me, all seeking peace through meditation.

If I were at home trying to do this by myself, I would have given up at the first moment I got distracted. In this safe space, I had the support of others who were also struggling. I was forced to sit through my discomfort until the gong sounded. When I couldn't concentrate anymore and looked up at those around me, I saw that everyone else was still meditating. So, I followed their lead. If they could do it, I could do it. I learned that you could meditate while moving—walking meditation, they called it. I learned that you could eat and meditate—a concept called mindful eating. I learned that the simple act of taking deep breaths was also a form of meditation. I learned that maybe this meditation thing could also be for me.

I started going to EBMC whenever I had the opportunity. One night a week, people of color sat together to meditate. I saw people meditating who looked like me. I saw meditation teachers who looked like me. Sometimes my hero, Alice Walker, the woman who wrote the book *The Color Purple,* would appear at these gatherings. Meditation was practiced by the very woman who taught me the definition of *womanist,* which has had a huge influence on my life. If you're not familiar, this fierce woman of wisdom defined it as follows:

1 From *womanish.* (Opp. of "girlish," i.e., frivolous, irresponsible, not serious.) A Black feminist or feminist of color. From the Black folk expression of mothers to female children, "you acting womanish," i.e., like a woman. Usually referring to outrageous, audacious, courageous, or willful behavior. Wanting to know more and in greater depth than is considered "good" for one. Interested in grown-up doings. Acting grown-up. Being grown-up. Interchangeable with another Black folk expression: "You trying to be grown." Responsible. In charge. Serious.

2 "A woman who loves other women, sexually and/or non-sexually. Appreciates and prefers women's culture, women's emotional flexibility (values tears as natural counterbalance of laughter), and women's strength.

   Sometimes loves individual men, sexually and/or non-sexually.

   Committed to survival and wholeness of entire people, male and female.

   Not a separatist, except periodically, for health. Traditionally universalist . . .

3 Loves music. Loves dance. Loves the moon. Loves the Spirit. Loves love and food and roundness.

4 Loves struggle. Loves the Folk. Loves herself. Regardless.

5 *Womanist* is to *feminist* as purple is to lavender.

When I first read this definition, I underlined so many words:

audacious
courageous
wanting to know more
responsible
committed to survival
wholeness
loves
REGARDLESS

I sat with it. It gave me power. It gave me presence. It gave me love. Love for myself. Love for others. Love for the experience of life itself. If Alice Walker meditated, I needed to meditate, and I stuck with it.

I started to realize that the mindfulness tools of meditation and breathwork that I was learning were extremely helpful to me outside of the vacuum of the yoga studio or meditation gatherings. When someone would say something offensive to me at work, I would think about all that I'd learned and what tool in my toolkit would be helpful. What could I do when I was so angry about a racist comment that I wanted to punch someone? What could I do when I was so nervous that my boss was going to fire me for a wrong step because I wasn't allowed the latitude that my white colleagues were? What could I do when someone touched my hair without permission? I realized that I could breathe in the moment to calm my nervous system. I realized that I could put a hand on my heart and allow myself to feel the pain after being harassed by the police, and that this simple action helped me feel just a little bit better. I realized that if I took five minutes to meditate about my intentions before going into an interview, I was able to really be the best version of myself.

I wanted to dig deeper. I wanted to understand the origins of these techniques. While white faces might be all over the media presenting these practices, the truth is that they originated in the East. People of color developed mindfulness practices thousands of years ago as a means of surviving. I wanted to learn from the source.

So, I packed my bags and took myself to India. I joke that I did the Black girl version of *Eat, Pray, Love,* but it really was the most transformational period of my life. With an open heart and an open mind, I went seeking. What else could I learn that could help me feel better in a world that just seemed to be getting harder and harder to navigate as a Black woman? What tools had generations of people been practicing that might help? I wasn't the first Black person to go to India for wisdom. Dr. Martin Luther King Jr. went to India in 1959, where he learned about Mahatma Gandhi's teachings. Dr. King wrote, "While the Montgomery boycott was going on, India's Gandhi was the guiding light of our technique of nonviolent social change." Dr. King found some powerful wisdom there. What was I to learn?

When I landed in Delhi, I was overwhelmed by all the action. I had been to big cities around the world before, but these crowds and the traffic were intense. I barely knew what to do with myself. I grew up in Washington, D.C., in the '90s, then the "murder capital" of America, and I thought of myself as street-smart. I knew to hold my purse tightly and watch my back for potential threats. But when a homeless boy with no legs grabbed my ankle as I was walking down the street, this Black girl didn't know what to do. *How was* this *the country known for yoga and meditation and reaching enlightenment?* I thought to myself.

And then it clicked. To remain grounded in the midst of this sort of chaos was a true superpower, and I wanted it. In fact, I needed it. I went to Kerala to do an intensive yoga teacher training with an emphasis on Ayurveda, one of the world's oldest holistic healing systems. I woke up in darkness to do early morning *kriyas*, cleansing rituals that had been used for thousands of years. Imagine drinking liters of a saltwater solution with the intention of vomiting every last substance in your digestive tract. With teachers watching to make sure we were doing it right and offering support, my fellow students vomited alongside me.

Yes, it sounded and looked weird. But everything I learned sounded and looked weird. Weird, and extraordinarily effective.

I'd never felt better in my life. I had to open my mind to the possibility that these ancient techniques had survived for so long because they worked. One of my teachers in India told me that he would never teach anything that he hadn't experienced himself. He called it lived experience, and he was right.

In the chapters that follow, I'm going to share some tools from my lived experience as a Black woman in America that have empowered my survival. No, I'm not going to suggest the vomiting exercise I just described. Instead I'm going to explain how the simple act of intentional breathing can clear your head and ground you during stressful experiences. I'm going to share how we, Black people, can take care of ourselves in a world where racial profiling is still part of our everyday existence, in a world where footage of police assaults on Black lives is now more a staple of the news cycle than a jaw-dropping event. I'm done with hearing "I can't breathe."

We, Black people, can breathe.
We do breathe.
We will breathe.

Key Points to Remember

- Mindfulness has been practiced by people of color around the world for thousands of years.

- Mindfulness is not just "white hippie stuff." Alice Walker, the author of *The Color Purple*, is an advocate of mindfulness and meditation. Dr. King found wisdom in Mahatma Gandhi's teachings. Mindfulness is not only *for* Black people, but it can help us during the hardest times.

Mindfulness Practice Toolkit

Mindfulness Practice 1: Three-Part Breath

When you're overwhelmed with emotions, and you need to feel more grounded:

1 Inhale slowly and deeply, and feel the air entering and moving through your throat, filling up your chest, and ultimately expanding your belly like a balloon. As you inhale, say to yourself, "Throat . . . chest . . . belly," as the air passes through each part of your body.

2 Exhale slowly, and feel your belly button come back toward your spine. Feel the air come up through your chest and back out through your throat. As you exhale, say to yourself, "Belly . . . chest . . . throat," as the air passes through each part of your body.

3 Repeat at least three times. If your emotions are extremely intense, repeat ten times.

Three-Part Breath

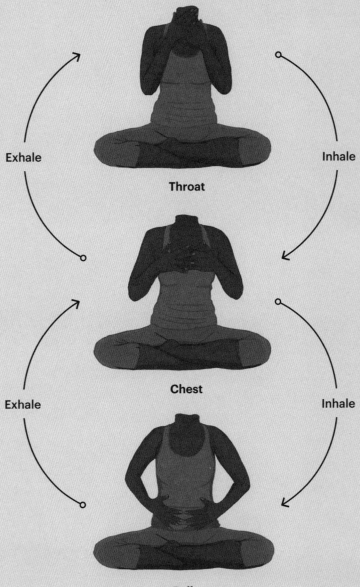

Exhale

Inhale

Throat

Chest

Exhale

Inhale

Belly

CHAPTER TWO

Bearing Witness to the Assault on Black Lives

No one ever taught me how to watch. I was taught what to do if I encountered them myself. "If you get stopped by the police, always address them as *sir*," I was told.

> Yes, sir.
> No, sir.
> Hands at ten and two on the steering wheel. Hands where you can see them.

Even as a girl I was taught this. My parents wanted me to be prepared. I knew what the police did to Black people. I heard stories from my neighbors, from my family, and from my friends. But no one ever taught me how to watch. I grew up in a time before smartphones and a time before Facebook, let alone Facebook Live. I grew up in a time before body cams were common, and the concept of mandatory body cams was unheard of. There was no footage of police brutality to be viewed. No one could imagine that we would ever need to know how to watch.

Fast forward to July 17, 2014. This was the first time that I remember needing this skill, and it wouldn't be the last. Headlines like NEW YORK MAN DIES AFTER CHOKE HOLD BY POLICE were all over the news. Eric Garner was murdered by Daniel Pantaleo, a New York City Police Department officer, during his arrest, and the video footage was everywhere. I, like many others, watched it. I watched a real-life murder on national television, and I will never be the same again. Do you remember where you were when you first heard about it? Did you watch?

Unfortunately, I've had many opportunities to figure out how to watch and make it through to the other side. To be clear, I'm still not okay. Every time, it hurts. Every time, I cry. But my mindfulness practice has helped me heal. It has helped me self-soothe, and I think it might be able to help you, too. So, what do I mean by *mindfulness*? And what does it have to do with police brutality?

Mindfulness means intentionally focusing your attention on what is happening in the present moment with curiosity and without judgment. When I was first exposed to the concept of mindfulness it took me some time to truly understand it, so let's dig in.

The first word I want to highlight is *intentionally*. Rather than playing a passive role, we are making a choice about how we engage. Have you ever been so immersed in a movie that you lost yourself for a bit and forgot that you were actually watching the movie rather than *in* the movie? In many stressful circumstances, we are similarly allowing ourselves to be drawn into the story. Mindfulness is setting the intention to watch instead.

Focusing your attention on what is happening. As the person watching, we are observing what is happening inside of us and around us. We are paying attention to our thoughts and our feelings. We are noticing what is happening in our physical bodies. We are noticing what is happening around us as well.

In the present moment. Our thoughts have a tendency to either get lost in the past or caught up in different versions of the future. There is something very powerful about being fully present. This moment is a gift, and we will never be right here, right now, again. Sometimes being right here, right now, can be painful. But these scars that we carry shape who we are. They make us wiser. They make us stronger. They help us teach our children all that we know.

With curiosity. I have always admired the curiosity that children bring to this world. They ask questions. They notice all the minute details that we as adults have become numb to. *Mindfulness* means taking in all the details—the colors, the shapes, the feelings, the textures—of what is happening inside us and around us.

Without judgment. It's so easy to judge ourselves. Have you ever had a thought, then been mad at yourself or ashamed for having that thought? These thoughts and feelings are temporary, and beating yourself up about them isn't going to help the situation. Without judgment, we observe ourselves as would an unbiased party. It's neither good nor bad. It just is.

Now let's see how we can apply this to the experience of witnessing police brutality. Although I hope that the police make permanent changes in how they treat us, if you are faced with footage of police brutality, here is how mindfulness can play a powerful role.

To Watch or Not to Watch? That Is the Question

I didn't pause to think about this decision when the Eric Garner footage came out. I was on autopilot. I clicked the video link without thinking. I wasn't paying attention to how I was feeling or what the impact might be. I was not intentional about how I handled it. But you can be.

There are many things that we don't have the opportunity to choose, and the ability to even make this decision is a privilege. So, why not make this decision while intentionally focusing our attention on our own well-being? There is no right answer, and you should do what feels right for you. However, you can be mindful about your choice. Here are five questions you can ask yourself when considering whether or not to watch.

Question 1: How am I feeling right now?

Pay attention to your current state. Are you ready to watch it? Or are you feeling fragile today?

Question 2: How will watching this impact me?

Harvard School of Public Health professor David R. Williams conducted a study of Centers for Disease Control and Prevention data that found that "every police shooting of an unarmed Black person was linked to worse mental health for the entire Black population in the state where that shooting had occurred for the next three months." Imagine how this effect is compounded, murder after murder. Although you might not be in the state where the shooting took place, it could still have a significant impact on your mental health. So, how can you be mindful of your own self-care when you make this decision?

Trauma, broadly defined as an emotional response to a distressing or disturbing experience, is very real. It can be incredibly overwhelming, and it can result in depression, anxiety, fear, shame, and so much more. As Black people, we might experience trauma from a huge range of things—microaggressions, macroaggressions, poverty due to systemic racism, and experiencing and watching police brutality over and over again.

It's possible that watching might trigger post-traumatic stress disorder (PTSD), not only from our own lived experience but from that of our ancestors. Epigenetic research suggests that trauma, and in our case the trauma of witnessing the abuse of our people and of being abused ourselves, is in our DNA. In Mark Wolynn's book *It Didn't Start with You,* he reveals that trauma causes a chemical change in our DNA, and this change can last for multiple generations. He shares a study of mice, which are often used because they share 99 percent of their genetic makeup with humans. Each time these mice were exposed to a cherry-blossom scent, they were given an electric shock. This resulted in changes to the brains, blood, and sperm of these mice. For example, their brains developed more smell receptors than average mice, as a form of protection. When these mice procreated, the next generation became jumpy and jittery just from smelling the cherry-blossom scent, even though they themselves were never given shocks like their parents. This stress response and genetic changes were seen in both the second and third generations. In additional studies of worms, researchers are finding similar effects for as many as fourteen generations.

Studies have shown that children of Holocaust survivors inherit the trauma symptoms of their parents, specifically lower cortisol levels. The cortisol hormone is critical to our ability to return to normal after trauma. The work of Rachel Yehuda, an epigenetic researcher at Mt. Sinai Medical School in New York, shows that descendents of Holocaust survivors inherit lower cortisol levels and as a result have a higher likelihood of experiencing anxiety disorders. Yehuda found similar results in children whose mothers were pregnant near the World Trade Center during 9/11.

These examples, whether in mice, worms, or human beings, describe trauma in one generation being passed down to the next. Imagine what this looks like when it is combined with trauma after trauma across multiple generations. Black people in America experienced the traumas of slavery, public lynchings during Jim Crow, KKK bombings of Black schools and churches during the civil rights movement, and much more. So, when we make the decision to watch the current-day oppression of our people, it could trigger PTSD caused not only by the present event but by all that happened before us.

Question 3: Where am I and who am I with?
Are you in the right environment for clicking on that link? Are you at work surrounded by white colleagues? Are you at home with your

partner, and have you made an agreement to watch it together and hold each other's hand? Deciding not to watch it right now doesn't mean you won't watch it, it means you're paying attention, and you might do it later, when you're ready. However, remember that it's completely okay not to watch at all. You are doing what's right for you, and that's all that matters.

Question 4: Do I have the time and space to take care of myself afterward?

If you think that watching will impact your ability to work or interact with others, ask yourself whether you will be able to take care of yourself after watching. Do you have to go to work right afterward? Do you have a long to-do list or errands to run? Consider delaying watching until you do have the time and space to process and heal.

Question 5: What are my reasons for watching?

The final question about being mindful in this decision is to think about your reasons to watch. For me, I have done it out of respect for, and to honor, the lives of those who we lost. Some want to be fully informed of the facts without the biases of secondhand information. Others might want to understand what the current risks are in this world to their own safety and that of their family members. If you are thinking about watching, what are your reasons?

Mindfulness While Watching

If you decide to watch, it can be traumatic, so it is very important to intentionally focus your attention on what is happening inside you. This will help you process, digest, and heal.

First, observe your body. Many have said that "our issues are in our tissues," especially in the world of somatic healing. Do you ever get a big, uncomfortable lump in your throat when you feel the urge to cry?

Have you ever been so stressed out that, without realizing it, your shoulders have crept up toward your ears? These are the issues in your tissues. If we aren't mindful of what's happening in our bodies, these effects can stay with us long after the traumatic event, and they build up over time.

The last time I watched footage of police brutality, all my muscles tensed. My stomach hurt. My forehead scrunched up. My eyes wanted to cry, but they couldn't. They were frozen. I had to remind myself to take deep breaths and breathe into these areas. I breathed into my stomach. I breathed into my forehead. It didn't change what happened, but it made watching it just a little bit more palatable, and my body was able to relax eventually.

When I watched George Floyd repeatedly say, "I can't breathe, I can't breathe," I literally stopped breathing. My natural bodily processes ceased to function. It wasn't until I noticed that I had stopped breathing that I could breathe once again.

When you watch these horrific events, pay attention to your heart rate, because it often increases. Notice any part of your body tensing up, and breathe there! If you can't focus the breath on anything in particular, just remember to be intentional about taking deep breaths. It will help calm you. I'm not saying this is easy. You're going to be in shock. But the breath will help. I promise.

Second, observe your thoughts. Be a witness to your thoughts without judgment. The nonjudgmental aspect is critical. There is already so much to handle that self-criticism does not have a place here. For example, when I watched Eric Garner get harassed by the police, he reminded me of my uncle. My uncle had a lot of run-ins with the police in the Bronx in the '80s, and he and Garner had similar mannerisms. I remember when my uncle was beaten up by the police and hospitalized for months. When I saw the Garner video, I thought, *I'm so happy my uncle was just hospitalized, not killed*. And then I felt guilty about it. I beat myself up inside because while my attention should have been on this terrible tragedy, I was thinking about my own family, and it felt selfish. In hindsight, I realize that a mindful approach would

have been to observe the thought, without judging myself, and realize that thoughts come and they go. They don't define me.

When we observe our thoughts, we are able to separate ourselves from them. We are not our thoughts, and this act of observation prevents us from getting lost in sometimes never-ending rabbit holes of torturous thoughts, cycling over and over in our minds.

What thoughts go through your mind as you watch? Notice them. Write them down. Writing them down helps release them from your psyche. You can't carry this weight around all the time. So, notice, observe, write it down, and exhale.

Third, observe your emotions. There is something powerful about being a witness to our emotions versus being consumed by them. When I watch, I experience so many emotions.

Sadness. I often get so sad that I can barely focus on anything that day. However, it is very helpful to acknowledge it. "I am experiencing sadness, and that is okay." It doesn't make the sadness go away, but it enables you to take action to address it.

Hopelessness. I sometimes experience a sense that things will never change. Then I start judging myself for this feeling. If my ancestors who experienced slavery were able to keep their hope alive, why am I so weak?

This is when a mindfulness practice should kick in. Without judgment: "I am experiencing hopelessness. This is temporary, and this doesn't make me a lesser person. This is just my experience at this moment."

Sometimes I feel no emotions at all. Emotional numbness. And that's when I'm judging myself the most. Cue mindfulness. Focusing my attention without judgment. Again, I have to say to myself, "I am experiencing numbness." From this perspective, I can recognize that numbness is likely a defense mechanism kicking in to say, "You can't handle any more of this." Rather than judging myself, I can see that perhaps this is me taking care of myself.

What emotions are you experiencing when you watch? Acknowledge them. Write them down. Try to observe them without self-judgment.

So, let's say you've got this observation part down. You now know how you're feeling, both physically and emotionally. You have observed your thoughts, and you're not judging yourself. You must be thinking, *Well, what do I do about it?*

Mindfulness after Watching

Immediately after watching, it's critical that you take time for yourself to process and heal. We have been brought up in a capitalist society that expects us to be productive at all times, and the easier thing to do is sweep any hard feelings under the rug and ignore them. I used to bury myself in work and pretend that I was okay. I now realize that the key to healing is to face these feelings head-on.

After watching the George Floyd footage, I placed a hand on my heart, closed my eyes, and took ten deep breaths. At first my body was so stiff. My heart was heavy. I couldn't take it anymore. *They keep killing us!* That's what I felt during the first breath. That's what I still felt at the second breath. By breath number 5, I started to soften. My hand had a tender touch, and I received this tenderness. I felt it not only on my body but in my soul. By breath number 7, I was able to calm down. By breath number 8, I knew that I was going to be okay. By breath number 9, I knew that change would come and that I needed to take care of myself. By breath number 10, I knew that we needed to take care of one another, and my exhalation was much longer than when I'd first started. I felt a sense of comfort.

When we witness violence inflicted on our people, our cortisol levels shoot up. Cortisol is our body's main stress hormone, and high cortisol levels can cause high blood pressure, headaches, anxiety, and a large range of other health problems. Studies show that self-soothing touch, such as placing a hand on one's heart, can reduce our cortisol stress response. This is why I was able to feel a sense of calm after my practice. I invite you to give it a try. Think of something that's causing you distress. Close your eyes, place a hand on your heart, and take ten

deep breaths. Observe how you're feeling physically and emotionally after each breath.

After this practice of placing your hand on your heart, journaling can be a powerful way to process the emotional roller coaster. When I opened my journal, the feelings poured out of me like the strongest waterfall. I just let it all out. Every last drop of it. Anger. Pain. Disgust. Disappointment. Sadness. Hopelessness. Helplessness. When I was finished, when there was nothing left to say, I took a deep breath and felt just a little bit lighter. It wasn't stuck inside me anymore. If you are ever overwhelmed with emotions, try writing it all down, and notice how you feel after releasing it onto the page.

After watching, you might feel helpless, like there's nothing you can do. This pain can be internalized and build up over time, especially after witnessing so many occurrences of police brutality against our community. When you feel this way, the ancient Tibetan practice of *Tonglen*, also known as Sending and Receiving, can be helpful. It involves receiving the pain of those who are suffering, and sending them love, warmth, and whatever else you think they might need.

After watching the George Floyd footage, I thought about the pain he was experiencing during his last nine minutes and twenty-nine seconds. I imagined what sort of emotions he could have been feeling during that time. I thought about his family and the pain and grief they must have been experiencing from the loss. When I inhaled, I breathed in their suffering. I held their suffering in my heart. Although there's no way to know what they felt, I did my best to see the world through their eyes. I tried, with intention, to feel their pain. Then, from that place of pain, I thought about what it is they might need right now. I thought about what words they might need to hear. I thought about what sort of prayer they might need. What sort of feeling might offer them a sense of comfort? And, from the most compassionate place within my being, I sent them what was needed when I exhaled. I breathed out as much love and compassion as I could. I sent them my prayers with my breath. I again inhaled their pain. It was heavy. It hurt. I embraced their suffering in my heart. And, when I exhaled, I breathed out what I thought they might need. I breathed out hugs. I breathed out warmth. I breathed out the whisper that they would get through this. I exhaled the energy of justice. I exhaled love.

We all try to empathize with suffering, but have you ever really sat down, put yourself in someone else's shoes, felt what you imagined they felt, and sent them what they might need? If not, I invite you to give it a try, from the most loving part of yourself.

The next step in this practice is to imagine all the people around the world who are suffering in this way. In this situation, I imagined all the Black people who had been attacked by the police, and all the families that had lost loved ones at the hands of the police. I repeated the process of breathing in their pain, and breathing out love and compassion. I exhaled prayers of healing.

I did this practice of Sending and Receiving for ten to fifteen minutes. I did it again the next day. And the day after that. I'm not saying that this practice will change what happened, but somehow it helped me energetically. It helped me feel like I was with them. It helped me feel better to know that my heart was sending them as much love and light as I could. From this place of love and compassion, I could then choose what to do, in terms of action toward justice and change.

If you try this practice, you should know that it can be pretty intense. I recommend being very proactive about self-care. If you are someone who holds tension in your neck like I do, I invite you to try rolling your neck from side to side. It can help release some of the pain that might still remain in your body after the experience. Exhale while lowering your chin to your chest; inhale and roll your right ear toward your right shoulder, hearing and feeling the cracks and rough spots along the way. Exhale back to center, with your chin to your chest, and inhale as you roll your left ear toward your left shoulder, feeling the spots that aren't so smooth on the journey on that side. Move more slowly through those tough spots—the areas that clearly need more of your attention. When I do this, I feel so much better.

None of this can change what happened, but if you're looking for ways to self-soothe, heal, and process, Sending and Receiving, followed by intentional self-care practices, can be a powerful tool.

Mindful Interactions with White People after Watching

At work. Remember that we are more affected than our white colleagues by these horrific events because they're happening to those in our community. We are expected to be fine, go to work, and pretend that everything is hunky-dory. I would have just seen a murder of a Black person on national television, and then I am in meetings where my colleagues act like it's business as usual. They act as if nothing had happened, so much so that I start to feel crazy.

We are expected to perform at our full capacity, which is unfair and often not possible. In these circumstances, I invite you to consider, if it works with your employment situation, unapologetically taking a sick day. Watching the brutal assault of a member of our community negatively affects our mental health and ultimately our physical health. Look up the physical symptoms of depression and trauma. According to the National Institutes of Health, depression can cause joint, limb, and back pain, gastrointestinal problems, fatigue, and changes in psychomotor activity and appetite. Research shows that trauma may cause gastrointestinal, cardiovascular, neurological, musculoskeletal, respiratory, and dermatological disorders; sleep disturbances; and urological problems. I certainly would consider this sick. If you can, take a day off! If you had the flu, you wouldn't think twice about it. The symptoms I just mentioned are real and must be addressed!

I know this isn't possible for everyone. Black people are killed so often in this country that if we skipped work every time it happened, we wouldn't have jobs.

Responding to "How are you?" I find this the toughest question to answer, especially after watching or even just hearing about police brutality and the loss of yet another member of our community. There is the real answer, and then there is the answer that comes out of my mouth. One of my biggest lessons around this question is to answer with intention. I used to answer on autopilot. We are trained to say, "I'm doing well, you?" regardless of how we are feeling. How many times have you answered "Good" or "Fine" when you were the opposite of that?

I am not saying that you should reveal your innermost secrets to everyone who asks. Some settings and some individuals do not foster a safe environment for honestly sharing how we are feeling. The mindfulness approach is to make a conscious choice. For me, this depends on my relationship with the person asking, and often my choice is about self-preservation. I say I'm fine because I don't want to deal with the repercussions. After the Ma'Khia Bryant murder, which happened on the same day as the Derek Chauvin guilty verdict for the murder of George Floyd, I responded that I wasn't doing well. That morning I was filled with so many emotions. I felt like I was supposed to be happy about justice being served, but instead I was in shock from watching a sixteen-year-old get shot. I was sad and disheartened that one guilty verdict doesn't mean that the world has changed. So, this is how the conversation went:

"How are you?" asked a white colleague at work.

"Honestly, I'm not doing very well. I just watched a Black teenager get shot by the police, and I'm really upset. It's like nothing has changed. Derek Chauvin was found guilty, but we are still getting murdered. And they are killing children!" I responded.

"I'm sorry to hear that. Yeah, I saw that in the news, but this one isn't like the others. She had a knife. If you're going to have a knife, well . . ." His pause implied that she deserved what came to her.

I practiced my breathing techniques as I observed heat and tightness in my chest. My mindfulness practice made me aware of my body, and I could feel the anger rising at lightning speed. I took deep breaths to keep my composure.

"I hear you, but who gets to decide who lives or dies?" I asked.

"Well, if you have a knife, you're going to experience the consequences. This happens to white people, too," he said very matter-of-factly. He proceeded to give me an example of a white person who wasn't murdered but was detained by the police.

I wanted to pull out statistics and data. I wanted to talk about the probabilities of this happening to him, a white man, versus someone with darker skin. But I was pissed. Frozen in regret for having brought it up.

"I just think about what to be teaching my kids. I want them to know that if they act like this, if they have knives, this is what will happen."

I didn't have the energy for a debate on ethical lessons for the next generation, so I just said this, with tears in my eyes:

"Did *you* see the footage?" He obviously hadn't. That shut down the conversation and I changed the topic because I couldn't handle it anymore.

Looking back, I don't regret bringing it up. I used to choose the answer that made white people more comfortable. "I'm good," I would say, so that they could feel good. I also didn't want to be the Debbie Downer friend or colleague that's known for talking about heavy things and depressing everyone. However, in hindsight, I would have done it a little differently. If you've ever been faced with a similar situation, here's how you can share how you're feeling, build awareness of an important issue in America, and still protect yourself from what can be an extraordinarily painful interaction:

"How are you?"

(Take an intentional deep breath so that you can be calm before responding.)

"I'm not doing well because I just watched a Black teenager get shot by the police, and I'm really upset. I don't want to talk about it, though. I'm sharing so you can be aware that, if I'm a little off today or this week, that's why." Period. Full stop.

If this happens at work, your colleagues can be more understanding about any potential impact on your job performance. If it happens in a social setting, your companions will know that perhaps you need some space. My responses are still a work in progress. Yours might be as well. The most important thing to remember is to make your responses intentional. Be mindful of what's good for you rather than giving a default response that feels good for others.

When you are the only Black friend of a "white ally." Many white people are trying their best to be good allies. But what does it mean to be a good ally? Although I do not have an answer for that, I can share some examples of attempts to be white allies and how to leverage a mindful approach in your response.

When anything about race and police brutality comes up in the news, I receive a plethora of texts and emails from white people, asking if I'm doing okay. I believe in my heart that most of them come from a place of genuine concern. Some of that concern might also be accompanied by a bit of guilt about their privilege and the acts of their ancestors.

However, I believe their intentions for the most part come from a loving place. That said, if you are their only Black friend, you tend to receive a high volume of these notes, because there are a lot of them and . . . well, one of you. Although it is well intended, I have found myself overwhelmed by this pity party to which I never RSVP'd. This is exacerbated when *only Black friend* actually means "only Black *acquaintance.*" In my head, I'm thinking, *Nice to hear from you, but the last time we spoke was ten years ago. Really? Am I the only Black person you could think of?*

So, what should you do? First, think about how you're feeling and how you're reacting to this outreach. For me, overwhelmed is usually the answer. Also exhausted, and, sometimes, plagued by obligation and guilt. Do you have the energy to respond? Do you feel like engaging? Do you feel obliged to be polite? To help them feel like they did the right thing, that they are good people, and that it's not their fault? Mindfulness is about observing these thought patterns and checking yourself when you notice them. The real question is, What can you do to prioritize your own well-being in these moments? How can you make *yourself* feel better?

Sometimes the white acquaintance from ten years ago will reach out and ask for my Black advice as a reaction to the news. Do you ever get questions like, "How can I raise my kids to be less racist?" or "What charities should I donate to?"

Here's a thought pattern that I started to observe in myself when inundated with these questions: *If I don't answer them, am I not doing my part to help change the world? If I don't answer them, who will?*

But exhaustion is real, y'all. If I did answer all of them, I might not have slept during all of 2020. So, the question remains the same: What can you do to prioritize your own well-being in these moments? That's mindfulness. It's paying attention to your own well-being.

You take care of you.

Key Points to Remember

- When deciding whether to watch footage of the assault on Black lives, consider asking yourself these five questions:

    a *How am I feeling right now?* Pay attention to your current state. Are you ready to watch it? Or are you feeling fragile today?

    b *How will watching this impact me?*

    c *Where am I and who am I with?* Is this the right environment in which to watch?

    d *Do I have the time and space to take care of myself afterward?* If you think that watching will impact your ability to work or interact with others, consider delaying watching until you do have the time and space to process and heal.

    e *What are my reasons for watching?*

- It's totally okay if you decide not to watch; however, if you do decide to watch, be intentional about the following while watching:

    - Observe your body.

    - Observe your thoughts.

    - Observe your emotions.

    - Take deep breaths, focusing the breath especially on areas of your body that are tense.

- Take time to process and heal after you watch. Consider journaling to get all your thoughts and emotions out, and find the space to practice some of the exercises in the Mindfulness Practice Toolkit.

- When interacting with white people after watching, be sure to ask yourself, "What can I do to prioritize my own well-being during this interaction?"

Mindfulness Practice Toolkit
Mindfulness Practice 2: Hand to Heart

When you're triggered by something awful, such as witnessing the assault on Black lives, and you need to self-soothe:

1 Close your eyes.

2 Place your hand on your heart.

3 Use a tender touch, and adjust the pressure to what feels just right for you in this moment.

4 Take ten deep breaths, receiving this tenderness and allowing yourself to be comforted.

5 Allow the breaths to grow deeper and longer.

Mindfulness Practice 3: Sending and Receiving (a.k.a. *Tonglen*)

When others are suffering and you want to send them love and support:

1 Find yourself a comfortable seated or lying-down position.

2 Inhale as fully as you can, and exhale with the intention of grounding yourself.

3 Inhale again, even more deeply this time, and exhale with the intention of grounding yourself.

4 Repeat a few more times until you feel more grounded and present.

5 Now focus on a person or group of people suffering.

6 Imagine experiencing their pain. See what they are seeing. Feel what they are feeling.

7 Now imagine what they might need right now. Maybe it's something they need to hear. Perhaps it's something they need to feel or something they need to know.

8 On your next inhalation, breathe in their pain. Feel what they feel.

9 On your next exhalation, send them what they might need right now with your breath.

10 Inhale and breathe in their pain. Live their experience.

11 When you exhale, send them what they might need, from the most compassionate part of you.

12 Repeat steps 8 through 11 for at least five minutes, or for as long as you feel comfortable.

Please note: This exercise can be very intense, and it is extremely important to be intentional about self-care after doing it. Please be gentle with yourself and take a more gradual approach to engaging with others afterward.

Mindfulness Practice 4: Neck Roll

When you've just experienced something very emotionally charged and need to release the tension:

1 Sit or stand with your back straight, shoulders lowered from around your ears.

2 Exhale and bring your chin to your chest, looking down.

3 Inhale and roll your right ear toward your right shoulder.

4 Exhale back to center, bringing your chin to your chest.

5 Inhale and roll your left ear toward your left shoulder.

6 Exhale back to center, bringing your chin to your chest.

7 Repeat steps 3 through 6 at least five times for each side, moving as slowly as you can. For the areas that feel tighter or might even crack, go even more slowly. Be as gentle as you can, and do what's best for your body.

CHAPTER THREE

Safety Is a Privilege

How do you feel when you encounter the police? Every time I see a police officer, my chest tightens, my entire body stiffens, and I look straight ahead, trying to be invisible, because I don't feel safe. It's ironic that the very people who are supposed to protect me make me feel like I'm in danger just by their mere presence.

Recent studies provide data that support what we've felt our entire lives. According to the National Academy of Sciences, "Black men are about 2.5 times more likely to be killed by police over the life course than are white men. Black women are about 1.4 times more likely to be killed by police than are white women." The media has historically focused on Black men and their safety; however, a *Washington Post* analysis finds that "Black women, who are 13 percent of the female population, account for 20 percent of the women shot and killed and 28 percent of the unarmed deaths." It's not safe for our men, and it's not safe for us, either!

Do you remember the first time you felt unsafe because of your race? I've felt unsafe for as long as I can remember. When I was seven years old and on a trip to a small town in North Carolina, a white man told my family that we belonged on the other side of the train tracks . . . "or else." That was my earliest memory of the fear that would pervade the rest of my life. When I was in sixth grade, I found a death-threat note in my backpack. I was at a predominantly white private school, and there weren't many people there who looked like me. The note had a drawing of a hanged stick figure, as in the Hangman game, with the blanks below filled out with YOU WILL DIE in capital letters. This hit me right in my gut when I read it. If my experiences with my classmates before had felt welcoming and friendly, perhaps I would have received it as a "joke," as the perpetrator said they had intended. However, this was not the case. I was worried that the mean girls at my school were going to gang up on me and that I would be helpless and alone when it happened. I felt like the black sheep, destined to a life of ostracism, and I didn't know what to do. Fear can be all-consuming. At age eleven, I was frozen and I was scared. So, I chose to do nothing and pretend it never happened. I held my fears inside and prayed that the whole situation would go away.

However, my parents found the note that night and were outraged. There was no question in their minds that this was race related, and they insisted that the school address it. At a class meeting, the teacher said, "Someone left this note in a Black student's backpack, and who-ever did it must come forward now!" I was so embarrassed, because "a Black student" was clearly me. There weren't any other options to choose from.

Looking back, I now understand that in addition to feeling that my physical safety was threatened I was also experiencing a lack of psychological safety as well. In Timothy Clark's book *The 4 Stages of Psychological Safety*, he defines psychological safety as "a condition in which human beings feel (1) included, (2) safe to learn, (3) safe to contribute, and (4) safe to challenge the status quo—all without fear of being embarrassed, marginalized, or punished in some way." Even before this incident, the clearly defined social cliques of rich white girls at my school definitely did not make me feel included. After it happened, I couldn't focus on learning or contributing because I felt like I had to watch my back at every moment. And, when the announcement was made in front of the whole class, I didn't just experience the "fear of being embarrassed, marginalized, or punished," I was *actually* being embarrassed, marginalized, and punished. Clark describes the consequences as "debilitating. It activates the pain centers of the brain."

If you have ever felt unsafe, either physically or psychologically, you should know that the pain you experienced is real and can negatively affect your health. Fear has a direct impact on your nervous system, which acts as the command center for your body. This system includes your brain, your spinal cord, and your body's extensive network of nerves. It controls your movements, your thoughts, and all the physical processes that happen without your conscious control, including breathing. Fear triggers your sympathetic nervous system, which flips your brain's limbic system into fight-or-flight-or-freeze mode. Your heart rate and blood pressure increase as you pump blood faster to deal with the stress. This physiological reaction happens when you think you are under attack, and you either choose to fight the attacker, run away, or freeze. We react this way instinctively, for survival. This is primal stuff! But constantly thinking we're under attack can cause all sorts of health problems, including the suppression of our immune system, chronic pain, heart disease, kidney disease, accelerated diabetes, inflammation, poor sleep quality, and much more. Chronic fear can also affect our emotional health, leading to feelings of helplessness, anxiety, mood swings, and obsessive-compulsive thoughts.

So, what can we do about it? We can't immediately change the world around us, but we can take actions to calm our nervous system so that we can feel better despite what can seem like a scary and dangerous world out there. The breath has been and continues to be the most powerful tool for me when I feel scared and unsafe.

Ever Had Trouble Sleeping?

Have you ever felt so anxious and scared that you couldn't sleep? I'm going to share a breathing technique that I used one night when I couldn't sleep because I was worried I would be the victim of a hate crime.

I had rented an Airbnb mountain cabin in Colorado with a friend of mine who is also a Black woman. Because of COVID-19 and its limited travel options, we decided to spend the Christmas holiday surrounded by nature, planning our meditation retreats and events for the following year. Less than twenty-four hours after arriving, on Christmas Day itself, we left the house to go for a hike and found a message on my car's back window: FUCK YOU in large letters. This was a private residence, and my car was parked in a private driveway. There was no reason for anyone to drive or walk up our driveway, and if they did by mistake, they could easily have turned around. From the driveway, you could see through the large windows, and we had left the curtains open so that we could enjoy the mountain views; whoever did this could see the two of us and our brown skin clearly through those windows.

I contacted the Airbnb host and asked whether hate crimes were a problem in the area and if we should be worried. He was surprised and offered to call the police. However, the police never came. They said they drove by and deemed it a "domestic matter." They never even came up the driveway to look at the car. They said that we could choose to press charges, but without an investigation, it was an empty offer because we would have no idea whom to press charges against. We thought about leaving the cabin and cutting our mountain getaway short, but we ultimately decided that we should stick it out.

There I was, lying in bed, eyes wide open, wondering if the hate-filled humans, who were likely nearby, would come back. What-if scenarios kept circling in my mind, and I couldn't sleep. Every time I heard a sound, I would jump up in fear that someone was trying to break in and attack us. Too many stories of Black people's houses set on fire during Jim Crow times haunted me, and I couldn't get my mind to stop torturing me with these awful possibilities.

It was then that I remembered a breathing technique that I'd learned in India called the Humming Bee Breath*. It's amazing for soothing the nerves and preparing the body for sleep. As a violinist, I love that this technique uses our own personal sounds and vibrations to heal. This idea that we can heal ourselves continues to surprise and comfort me, even though I've been using this and many other self-healing tools for years.

This is what to do if you can't sleep: Sit up in bed, with your back straight so that you can breathe deeply. Plug your ears with your thumbs to block out any outside sounds. Cover your eyes with your fingers to block out any visual distractions. Inhale deeply through your nose; then, with a long, slow exhalation, make a humming sound while keeping your mouth closed. The shorter version of this exercise lasts for ten breaths. If you're having a really rough night, increase it to twenty breaths. If you lose count, be gentle with yourself and calmly begin counting again from the beginning. I invite you to give it a try and see how it feels.

For me, it was like creating my own personal sensory-deprivation chamber as I immersed myself in the sound of my own voice. At first it was weird to hear that sound inside my head. It almost felt the way sounds do underwater. You can hear them, but they have a certain unique texture. As I eased into the exercise, and continued to hum, I could feel my shoulders sink from around my ears. I could feel my heart slow down. I could feel muscle by muscle start to soften. Muscles I didn't even know were tight started to loosen up. With every breath, I focused on that space between my eyebrows that I had learned was called the third eye, access to my intuition and inner wisdom. I started to be able to find comfort in this space, in this sound, in this vibration—my vibration.

When I counted twenty breaths, I removed my thumbs from my ears and uncovered my eyes. I could feel the coolness of the air inside my ears, like a refreshing glass of lemonade on a hot summer day. My breaths continued to be long and deep. Calmer. More at peace.

* This technique is inspired by a practice called *Bhramari* in Sanskrit.

Humming Bee Breath

Plug your ears

Cover your eyes

Inhale

Long hum as you exhale

As if I had just journeyed to a place where everything was going to be alright. And I returned with the wisdom and knowledge that it was true, even here, in this mountain town where I did not feel welcome.

The Humming Bee Breath was a godsend after hours of insomnia. I was so grateful that it came to me at that moment, and I was so grateful that I had learned it. Several studies show that this particular technique lowers your blood pressure and heart rate, which is helpful as we try to sleep. Studies also show that the Humming Bee Breath stimulates the parasympathetic nervous system. Do you remember the sympathetic nervous system I described earlier, our fight-or-flight-or-freeze reaction? The parasympathetic nervous system, known as the rest-and-digest nervous system, helps counter the work of the sympathetic nervous system after stressful situations. It acts like the brakes on a car and slows us down, reducing our respiration and heart rate and allowing us to conserve energy. We need both nervous systems to regulate our lives, and when we are under extreme duress, if we are mindful that it's happening, we have the power to counter this stress by proactively stimulating our parasympathetic nervous system with our breath. That night in the cabin in the woods, my mind was torturing me with all sorts of awful possibilities about what might happen. The Humming Bee Breath helped me calm down. If you are ever caught in a swirl of anxiety and "what-ifs" about your safety or that of your loved ones, I invite you to give this a try.

There are many everyday situations in which we feel unsafe. In this case, I was trying to have a peaceful vacation. I met some Black people who told me that someone had called the cops on them when they were hiking. What were they doing wrong? Hiking, apparently. Ahmaud Arbery was just jogging, trying to get some exercise, and we all know what happened to him.

There is another environment that we might not immediately think of as unsafe, but I hear about it over and over again—the doctor's office.

How Safe Do You Feel at the Doctor's Office?

Have you ever gone to the doctor and felt like they weren't taking you seriously? If so, it's not all in your head, and you are not alone. A study published in the *Proceedings of the National Academies of Science* shows clear racial bias in pain assessment and treatment recommendations, because "Black Americans are systematically undertreated for pain relative to white Americans." If a Black person and a white person go into the emergency room with the same type of broken leg and similar pain levels, the Black person is significantly less likely to get any medication to ease the pain. The same study surveyed white medical students and residents and asked them whether they believed statements such as "Black people's nerve endings are less sensitive than white people's nerve endings" (which is clearly false). They also asked participants to imagine how much pain white or Black people would feel in situations such as getting their hand slammed in a car door and what their suggested treatments would be.

Almost half the white medical students endorsed these false beliefs. That means that the white doctors of the future are only 50 percent likely to believe Black people's pain and offer adequate treatment. Essentially, the doctor's office has only a 50 percent chance of being safe for Black patients.

Until 2017, nurses were *taught* that Black people "report higher pain intensity than other cultures." They learned that we exaggerate our pain and that we're not really feeling what we say we are. This was in active print in a Pearson nursing-school textbook. There are more than 4 million nurses in the United States, and I can't imagine how many of them were influenced by this when engaging with Black patients.

So, what can you do if your doctors or nurses aren't giving you the treatment you deserve? In these situations, if you're like me, the pain you're experiencing, coupled with the frustration and anger about how you're being treated, might rile you up so much that you can't think straight. The breath can help.

A few years ago, I went to my doctor because I was experiencing such extreme fatigue that it was affecting my ability to work. I'm usually a really high-energy person, but during this period my body ached and I could barely get off my couch. My doctor told me that it was probably nothing and that it would go away soon. A week later I started to experience heart palpitations while walking down the street. If you've never felt this before, let me tell you, it is scary. I felt my heart start changing its rhythm, skipping beats, doing all sorts of weird things. I went to a different doctor, and she had the same response. "Don't worry about it. It'll pass!" she said, smiling. Meanwhile, my heart was racing and curse words were flying through my head as I was screaming to myself, *Why won't she believe me?*

This was my fight-or-flight-or-freeze reaction (a.k.a. my sympathetic nervous system) going crazy. Have you ever looked back at a doctor's visit and wished you had asked more questions and challenged what they said? That's what happened to me that day. I basically froze.

However, when she left the room for a few minutes, I pulled it together. I began to practice a technique called Straw Breathing. Although it's traditionally done with an actual straw, you can do a version without it, because who has a straw on them at all times? Here's how it works: Inhale deeply through your nose. Purse your lips as if you were drinking through a straw. Exhale as slowly as you can through pursed lips.

After just three of these breaths, I could feel myself relax. This technique also stimulates the parasympathetic nervous system, and I could feel my rational brain come to my rescue. Straw Breathing allowed me to conjure up the calmest code-switching voice that I could. When the doctor returned, I insisted that there must be some tests that could determine what the problem might be. Turns out I had Lyme disease! If left untreated, it could have caused chronic joint inflammation, neurological and cognitive deterioration, and who knows what else. I was immediately put on an antibiotics protocol, and a few months later I was back to my old energetic self!

If you try this technique, you'll notice that exhaling with your lips

Straw Breathing

Inhale

Exhale through pursed lips

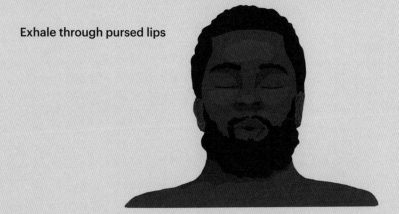

pursed makes a gentle and audible sound, which might seem weird to do in public. Although I did it when my doctor left the room, what if your doctor doesn't give you that opportunity? If you're wary of doing things like this in front of people, especially at the doctor's office, I say do it anyway! If 50 percent of the time they are not going to believe you about your pain, isn't it worth the risk of them thinking you're weird, just to increase your chances of getting the medical treatment that you deserve? If they do hear you breathing and ask what you're doing, tell them that you're Straw Breathing to stimulate the parasympathetic nervous system because their dismissing your symptoms is causing a stress response. What do you think they will say to that?

Dreaming of a Better World

Your day-to-day reality can be filled with a lot of challenges to your physical and psychological safety, and if you sit in this reality for too long, you might end up just accepting that this is the way it's always going to be. But we have tools to help us manage these everyday threats, from FUCK YOU written on cars to death threats in backpacks. We will not accept this as the status quo. We must continue to dream of a better world. Harriet Tubman said, "Every great dream begins with a dreamer. Always remember, you have within you the strength, the patience, and the passion to reach for the stars to change the world." We are the dreamers, and change will come.

One tool that can help you dream is visualization. Artist Natasha Marin's exhibit *Black Imagination* asked Black participants in Chicago to "imagine a world where you are safe, valued and loved." Marin later published a book containing some of the responses, and this one, from Laura Lucas of Seattle, Washington, particularly resonated with me:

> You don't talk about moving because I bought the house next to yours. You don't try to touch my hair, without asking, without

saying hello or even speaking when I walk past you. You don't expect me to do all the work that no one else feels like doing. I'm just out in the world, being myself without fear, shimmering through a star-filled sky.

When I first heard about this exhibit, it struck me that I had never imagined such a thing. Having spent most of my life not feeling safe, valued, and loved, it was such a foreign concept to dream up. Closing my eyes and really sitting with this, truly imagining and living it, was extraordinarily powerful. I imagined feeling free to go wherever I wanted without fear. There are so many beautiful places in this country, but I'm genuinely scared I might get shot by a white nationalist in some of them, so I'll never go. I imagined feeling like I could pursue all my dreams and that anything was possible. If I encountered any pitfalls, someone would be there to catch me. This really made me smile. I've never truly felt this way. Resting in this vision, in this experience, felt like hot chocolate and marshmallows on a snowy day. Cozy. Warm. After sitting with this visualization, I wrote it down. Now, every time I'm not feeling safe, or valued, or loved, I read what I wrote, and I know that change will come.

Close your eyes and imagine a world where you are "safe, loved, and valued." What do you see?

Key Points to Remember

- If you ever feel unsafe, either physically or psychologically, the pain you are experiencing is real and can have a direct impact on your health.

- Fear for your safety or that of a loved one can cause your mind and body to spring into fight-or-flight-or-freeze mode, which is your sympathetic nervous system kicking into gear—faster heart rate, higher blood pressure, rapid breathing, etc.

- We can't immediately change the world around us, but through the breath, you can restore a sense of calm so that you can handle any stressful situation with a clear head.

- We will not accept the status quo. We are dreamers, and change will come.

Mindfulness Practice Toolkit

Mindfulness Practice 5: Humming Bee Breath[*]

To calm down when you are having trouble sleeping or your mind is spiraling:

1 Plug your ears with your thumbs, without bending your earlobes and cartilage.

2 Cover your eyes with your fingers.

3 Inhale through your nose.

4 Exhale with a long humming sound. Make the exhalation as long and slow as you can.

5 Focus on the space between your eyebrows.

6 Repeat for ten to twenty long, deep breaths, or for five minutes, if you have the time.

[*] This practice should not be attempted if you are pregnant or have epilepsy, chest pain, or an active ear infection.

Mindfulness Practice 6: Straw Breathing

When you get really frustrated because you don't feel heard, at the doctor's office or elsewhere:

1 Inhale deeply through your nose.

2 Purse your lips like you are drinking through a straw.

3 Exhale as slowly as you can through pursed lips. If you have an actual straw, slowly exhale through the straw.

4 Repeat for three breaths, if you don't have much time. Continue for five minutes, if you have more time.

Mindfulness Practice 7:
Visualization: A World Where You Are Safe, Valued, and Loved

When you are feeling overwhelmed and perhaps disheartened by how unsafe this world can be:

1 Put your phone on Do Not Disturb mode and set a timer for five minutes.

2 Close your eyes.

3 Take a few deep breaths.

4 Imagine a world where you feel safe, valued, and loved. Imagine you are watching a movie about this experience. What are you seeing? What are you doing? How are you feeling? Be in the experience.

5 When the timer rings, write down in your journal all that you saw and experienced.

6 Revisit what you wrote the next time you are feeling down.

CHAPTER FOUR

Shopping While Black

My mother always told me to fix myself up before going to any store.
Makeup. If I'm opting for casual, then I should wear my "nice" casual
clothes. "Look presentable," she would say, "because you never know
how they are going to treat you." This is what it can be like to go shopping as a Black person. Although most of us think of this as common
sense based on stories we've heard from friends and family or our own
personal experiences, there is data to support it. A Gallup survey shows
that Black adults are five times less likely than white adults to be treated
with courtesy and respect. Let me repeat that.

Five times less likely than white adults
to be treated with courtesy and respect.

This isn't a subtle difference. Our reality is starkly different.
Constantly being treated differently can have a long-term effect on
our psyche and our well-being. David R. Williams, professor of African

and African American studies and sociology at Harvard University, explains that "reports of discrimination are linked to worse mental health" and we see "higher levels of everyday discrimination linked to increased obesity. We see it linked to a broad range of health out-comes . . . incident diabetes, incident cardiovascular disease, incident breast cancer . . . as well as a range of other underlying indicators of chronic disease, such as inflammation. So, the evidence is clear: These little indignities add up and take a toll on individuals."

I'm a rock climber, and a couple years ago I went to an outdoor-gear shop to buy some rock-climbing shoes. I went during an off-peak time so I wouldn't have to wait. I knew exactly what I wanted to try on because I had done thorough research beforehand. This particular afternoon, there were only three customers in the entire store. As I entered, I went straight to the rock-climbing-shoe section, as if on a mission. The man working there had just brought over some shoes for a white couple to try on.

"Excuse me," I said, trying to get his attention. At this point the man wasn't doing anything at all, just standing there idle. He didn't respond.

I waited a bit and continued pretending to look at shoes, just to give him a second to be present and do his job. In my view, his job was to approach browsing customers and ask if they needed any help. This did not happen.

"Excuse me," I said again, more loudly. Perhaps he didn't hear me the first time. No response.

"*Excuse me,*" I now said, very clearly trying to get his attention. At this point I was visibly annoyed. Yet, still, no response. Has this ever happened to you? Have you ever felt completely ignored when trying to get help at a store?

Finally the woman of the white couple whom he had just helped said to him, "I think this woman needs some help." Like a loyal dog who listens only to his master's commands, he immediately asked me if I needed anything. As the white couple watched, he did follow through and get me the shoes I wanted to try on. I figured out which ones

I wanted, then I went to the competing store across the street to buy the shoes. They weren't going to get any of my business!

Bad service at a store is one thing; however, racial profiling takes the shopping experience to an entirely new level. In April 2021, eleven-year-old Ja'Mari Oliver, a Black student in fifth grade, walked into a Safeway in San Francisco to buy a sandwich while his mother waited in the car. After he paid for the sandwich and was on his way back to his mother, he was stopped by a security guard, who told him to put the sandwich down, accusing him of shoplifting. He showed the security guard his receipt, but he wasn't allowed to leave until the store manager cleared him. The fifth-grader said that the experience made him sad. He shared, "I felt scared like something could have happened. I was just crying."

When he left the store in tears, his mother said, "I was very hysterical with the whole situation that was taking place." She went into the store to talk to the manager. They said they would talk to the security guards and offered her a $25 gift certificate. This experience will likely stay with her son for the rest of his life, and how much is this pain worth to Safeway? A whopping $25.

When you're a child, they call the security guards. When you're an adult, they call the police. After I spent $220 at Raley's, a regional grocery chain in Sacramento, California, a store employee called the police on me. I was moving across the country and had decided to make the journey a camping road trip through the beautiful national parks along the way. My car was packed to the brim with my personal belongings as well as all the camping gear for me and a friend who'd joined me on the trip. We were going to be in the wilderness without much access to stores, so we stopped to buy food and a cooler. As my friend and I were playing a challenging game of Tetris trying to reorganize the trunk to fit in all that we had just bought, we heard sirens, and a police SUV pulled up in a frenzy and parked so as to block us from leaving.

"Ma'am, did you buy those groceries? We have a witness cashier that says that you took several items without paying for them," said a six-foot-tall white policeman in full uniform, accompanied by his partner.

"Excuse me?" I said, shocked and horrified at the accusation. After the officer repeated himself, I said to my friend, "Can you pull out our receipt?"

My heart rate shot up. I had a terrible feeling in my gut that this was going to be "my turn." My uncle had been beaten up by the police. I had friends in high school who had been locked up without any evidence, and I was scared. It was at this moment that I realized I had to keep my cool, for my own survival. As the two policemen began to search my car, I started breathing deeply in and out of my belly. The Belly Breath is the number-one tool I've learned for coping with moments of duress. I knew that any small move could turn this situation into direct physical pain for me, and I needed to keep it under control.

"Breathe in through the belly. Breathe out through the belly," I told myself silently.

In, I thought as I inhaled and felt my belly expand as much as it could.

Out, I thought as I exhaled and felt my belly come back toward my spine.

In. Out.

In. Out.

I needed my heart rate to slow down. I needed to stay calm and not make a false step.

"Focus on the breath," I kept repeating to myself. I was trying to get my parasympathetic nervous system to kick in and do its job, because I desperately needed it. At that moment, on this ninety-degree day with the scorching sun on my face, with the backs of my thighs burning as I was forced to sit on the hot metal of my back bumper, I needed it to kick in. I needed to stay calm.

And it worked.

"Ma'am, what's this?" the policeman asked while holding the receipt.

"It's a cucumber; an English cucumber," I said calmly. "It's on the receipt," I added.

Belly Breath

"Chips; okay, that's on there," he said.

"Mushrooms? What kind of mushrooms are these? Oh, yeah, okay, I see them on here."

This went on for quite a while, until he said, "Do you have any deli meats? You were seen spending quite a bit of time in the deli section."

"I'm a vegetarian," I said.

"Actually, she's a vegan," my friend said.

"I think she got some soppressata, but that's it because, as she said, I'm actually a vegan so there's literally no meat but that," I said.

I had been stuck near the deli section trying to find plant-based options and struggled. Everything had cheese in it, and there wasn't anything tofu- or otherwise plant-based within sight. So, yes, I did remember standing there for a while, thinking I should have gone to Trader Joe's.

After they searched all the grocery bags, they continued to search the rest of my car. Imagine all your things spread across the concrete of a store parking lot. Sleeping bags. Tents. Clothing. All my bags were opened and ransacked in this search for meat.

"Am I going to find anything in *this*?" one of them asked as he picked up my reusable grocery bag, which I had been using as a purse. He acted like he was an amazing detective who had just cracked the case.

"I really don't know what to tell you, Officer. There is no meat in this vegan's car," I reiterated calmly, breathing in through my belly, breathing out through my belly.

The officer said that they had us on the surveillance camera, so if we took anything they would know. "You better be honest," he said sternly.

He went back into the store, I assumed to watch the video, while his partner kept a watch on us. The woman who'd accused us refused to come out to the parking lot to do it in person, the officer said.

"What's your Social Security number?" he asked. "Do you have any tattoos?" Apparently this was for identification if at a later date there was a search for us, he explained.

Finally after several hours of harassment, and losing any hope of arriving at our campsite that day due to the dwindling daylight, they let us go, with a warning that there could be a warrant out for our arrest if they were to learn anything later. These are the final words I remember hearing before starting the process of gathering my things and repacking my car:

"We're just not used to seeing people with reusable grocery bags around here," the officer said.

"In San Francisco, they are pretty common," I replied. "It's just that this seems to happen quite a bit to people who look like me," I said, with sweat glistening on my brown skin in the hot sun.

"Sorry ma'am, we are just doing our due diligence. We're just doing our job."

We all know what "just doing our job" can mean. If you remember nothing else from this book, remember the Belly Breath, especially when you get stopped by the police. It could literally save your life. I was relieved that we were able to leave this situation unscathed. I was grateful that the Belly Breath helped keep me from giving them any reason to hurt us. But, damn, I couldn't help thinking, *What the f&*^!*

I woke up the next morning in my sleeping bag at a campsite much closer than the one we had originally planned on, given the hours of delay that the police had caused. I was fixated on what happened, and I could feel the rage building inside of me. A teacher once explained to me the importance of naming the emotion that I was feeling; she said that by naming it I would be able to separate myself from the emotion and take a step back. By naming it I would be aware that I was experiencing this emotion, but I was not the emotion itself. I pondered this in my tent. *Breathe*, I told myself. *I am experiencing anger. I am experiencing rage.*

I let myself feel it. I took some deep breaths and thought about what to do next. *They will not get away with this*, I thought. *This will not go unaddressed*. Having acknowledged what I was feeling, I was able to access the rational part of my brain that could take action. I was able to find some clarity amid my heightened emotions. Without internet access, I pulled out my laptop and typed this open letter to the grocery chain. I would send it when we got to the next town with connectivity.

Dear Raley's:

At 11:11 a.m. on July 11, 2018, I spent $220 at store 239. In the parking lot, the police searched my car and my personal belongings, accusing my friend and I of shoplifting. They told us that our cashier (Operator 681161) saw us steal. There was no evidence of this theft. All of the grocery items were on the receipt. The police diligently went through every item. The surveillance videos showed that we paid for everything. What sort of message should I and your customers take away from this? Why did Operator 681161 think we had stolen anything when she herself checked us out, and literally watched us pay for all of the items? I am a Black woman with a Harvard MBA. My friend is an Asian woman and a corporate lawyer. And we chose to spend money at your establishment. Should we, and others that look like us, make different choices going forward?

What sort of training do you have in place that makes this sort of behavior acceptable? What policies do you have around the treatment of your customers, especially those that might look a bit different than your employees? What is an acceptable basis for shoplifting accusations in your stores? Is it in your employee handbook to call the police and have your customers searched, without even talking to the accused first? What procedures do you have in place?

As a vegan, it's ironic that they were searching for deli meats. Also, I would have spent less time in the deli section if there were a larger plant-based-food selection in your stores. Not that I have any desire to give you any more of my money, but for those that continue to shop with you, I have a few requests:

First, please discontinue the practice of having police accuse and search your customers, especially those that buy a lot of groceries (and are people of color).

Second, please consider re-evaluating your company policies and employee-training procedures to ensure all of your customers are treated with dignity, regardless of ethnicity, religion, socioeconomic status, or sexuality.

Lastly, it would be great if you could expand your selection of plant-based-food options. You will be doing a great service to the health of Americans and to the longevity of our planet.

Sincerely,
Z. Clarke

The letter received enough attention on social media and in the news for the CEO of the company to offer an apology. The American Civil Liberties Union (ACLU) offered its help with negotiations as I tried to get Raley's to make some drastic changes to their policies and their training. I did not have any experience with these sorts of negotiations, and I felt manipulated when the CEO repeatedly tried to get me on the phone without the ACLU lawyers. He was an older, rich, white man in power, and I'd had so many experiences with people like him in the workplace acting like bulldozers. I was scared, I was fragile, and I felt unequipped.

What I wanted most was for this never to happen to anyone who walked into Raley's stores ever again. Although I couldn't claim to have the silver bullet for making this happen, I had some suggestions involving mandatory implicit- and explicit-bias training, along with cultural-sensitivity training, for all staff; hiring a diversity consultant to evaluate and make recommendations on the company's discrimination policies; and creating an accountability structure to monitor customer interaction with the police and random checks on employees for quality control. This process was extraordinarily stressful because it was all happening while I was on a camping road trip. Imagine being at the top of a mountain in Montana, holding the phone at just the right angle to get reception, and having to negotiate such emotionally charged issues.

The lowest point for me was a Facebook message I received from an employee at the corporate office who was so disturbed at how this had been handled that they felt I needed to know what was happening behind the scenes. First, they told me to ask on what date the company had added antidiscrimination language to its policies and employee handbook. The corporate team told me that they already had such language, but the inside scoop was that they had added it the day all this happened so that they would be ready for the PR backlash. This just felt like your average big-company shadiness. Not surprising; definitely disappointing. But what brought me to tears was their next point. My informant told me there was an office pool about what I would ask for, with many assuming my motivation was a large sum of cash. An envelope held their money and their guesses.

I will never forget the moment when I learned that this incident, which was already traumatizing in itself, was actually just a big joke to the folks in charge. Yes, people make mistakes. There was no way to change what had happened in the past. However, they did have the power to influence the present and the future. Their handling of this speaks a lot to their values, but, more than just *their* values, on a more personal note it speaks to how much *I* was valued—in this case, not at all. I felt utterly worthless, like there wasn't a place for me in this world. That no matter what I did, no matter how many fancy degrees I had, no matter how much I tried to prove to white America that I did belong here, I was, and would always remain, worthless in their eyes.

I was a hot mess. My tears were so powerful that I couldn't move. My entire being just didn't want to be. I called close friends, seeking solace, but there was only so much of "I'm sorry that happened" that I could take. And then I remembered the mindfulness technique of RAIN, an acronym developed by mindfulness teacher Michele McDonald, which has since been expanded upon by many teachers and psychologists, including Tara Brach in her book *Radical Compassion*. Brach's interpretation has really stuck with me, and in this moment of despair, hopelessness, and sadness, it was the medicine that I needed. If you ever experience something so overwhelming that you feel like you don't know what to do, I invite you to practice this technique:

Recognize

Allow

Investigate

Nurture

The *R* in *RAIN* Is for *Recognize*

Recognize how you're feeling. Acknowledge that you are not okay. As Black people, we are expected to always be strong, or to at least look like we are strong. But you might not feel strong in these moments.

This concept of recognizing and acknowledging how I was feeling did not come naturally to me. Like many Black people, I was taught never to show weakness. My father quoted Sun Tzu's *The Art of War* a lot when I was a child: "Appear weak when you are strong, and strong when you are weak." The latter was so deeply engrained in me that my reflex was to always appear strong, even to myself. I wouldn't admit that I was struggling, even when no one was around. But, after years of unlearning old habits, here I was, recognizing that I was not okay. I was finally brave enough to accept that truth. I wrote down everything that I felt in my journal. It was like vomiting all of the ickiness that had ever existed in the world, directly onto that page.

When you experience overt racism, more subtle microaggressions, or anything else that triggers you, this first step of recognizing how you feel and naming the emotions is critical to your healing.

The *A* in *RAIN* Is for *Allow*

If you're like me, you might have learned to sweep any difficult emotions under the rug. I grew up in a household where we didn't talk about feelings. In fact, if I told my father I was sad, I would get slapped in the face. If I showed any tears at all, they would be met with a stern, "You want something to cry about?" So, I would try to contain the big lump in my throat for as long as possible until I could run to my room and cry. And even in my room, all by myself, I tried to hold the tears back because weakness was not acceptable. Learning to allow the feelings to be there was a huge departure from my upbringing. After talking to my kind Raley's informant, I let myself feel all of the things. I cried and cried. I honored these emotions with the space to exist. I let them feel like they belonged. I finally believed—like, really believed—that it wasn't wrong to feel these things. That they had a place, and I would let them have this place.

Have you ever truly allowed yourself to feel all your feelings? It can be a powerful and cathartic release.

The *I* in *RAIN* Is for *Investigate*

Once you really spend time with these feelings, begin to investigate where in the body you are feeling them. Be a detective, and describe the details of the experience. My attention immediately went to my heart. My heart felt like an enormous stone. Rock solid. So heavy that it weighed down my entire body. Aching. The weight of it caused an aching pain that felt like a never-ending curse. Raw. I felt like I was so exposed and the pain penetrated even more deeply because I had no protection. Then there was my stomach. My stomach felt like I had just been stabbed with a sharp sword. It felt like my organs had been ripped out and I was left with an open wound, gushing blood, except that there was no more blood to shed. Again, raw. My jaw was clenched with all this pain. My face scrunched up as the tears continued to flow. And my breath was fast and short. I could barely breathe between the tears. I was shaking. When you experience something like this, take time to really sit with every sensation. Observe every detail of what's happening.

From here, once you are fully aware of everything that is going on with you, it is time to proceed to the last step.

The *N* in *RAIN* Is for *Nurture*

From this place of vulnerability, ask yourself what you need in order to feel better. For me, from this place of pain and clenching and shaking, I asked myself what I needed to hear or to believe or to know that would make me feel better? At first this was really tough. I didn't know. I felt like nothing could make me or this feel better. So, I sat with it. I closed my eyes, I sat with the pain, and I asked my heart, I asked my stomach, I asked my jaw, "What do you need?"

And slowly it came to me. I needed to know that the world was not evil. I needed to know that I *did* matter. I needed to know that the world *would* change. I needed to know that I had the strength to get through this. I needed to know that I was going to be okay, and that future generations were going to be okay also.

I placed one hand on my heart and the other hand on my stomach. I felt the warmth from my hands provide a sense of comfort. Something about the tenderness of my own touch helped me calm down. I had learned about this concept of touch healing from my Reiki training, and it felt so good. I could finally breathe a little more deeply.

I called upon my higher self. I called upon my ancestors. I asked them for guidance and help, and I allowed myself to hear and feel the nurturing words that I needed. I felt like a baby being rocked by its loving mother.

"It's gonna be okay, baby. You're gonna be okay."

"Love will prevail, honey. It just takes time."

"We're with you, baby. You are not alone. We have your back."

And then I gave myself a hug. I crossed my arms at the elbows and took hold of the opposite shoulder blades, took a deep breath, and squeezed myself so tight. I exhaled.

Only you know what you need, but you can't receive it unless you ask yourself for it. It might be different every time, but it's important to make the space to identify what you need so that you can offer it.

I wish I could say that I did this practice of RAIN once and everything was all better, but the truth is that I had to repeat it over and over again throughout the negotiations. The grocery chain leadership team thought it was enough to issue a public written apology to me and send a letter to all employees reminding them to review their discrimination policies. The letter had no mention of what had happened to me and no specifics about calling the police or harassing Black shoppers. Eventually they agreed to in-person interactive training for the executive team on implicit bias. When I pushed back because it was the frontline employees in the actual stores that called the police, I received resistance. I think they got down to the store managers, but never to the level of the employee that called the police—unless you count the thirty-minute go-through-the-motions online training they implemented. I've been through those before. You can be on YouTube or talking on the phone, and all you have to do is click through the module to get it marked as complete. Not exactly the most impactful, but I give them an A+ for "checking the box."

I did get them to hire a diversity consultant, and the CEO called me a year later to tell me that their leadership team was now 50 percent female. I responded, "Congrats on gender equality, but how does that prevent future harassment of Black shoppers at your stores?" He then told me they had hired a Black woman for the leadership team. Kudos on the hire, but at this point I was emotionally exhausted. I was clearly not going to convince them to make any drastic changes, and I had to prioritize self-care, so I let it be. Months later I received a call from a lawyer representing Black security guards at the same grocery chain who had been instructed to follow Black shoppers with full carts around the store. They were called the *n*-word and fired for speaking up against these instructions. The grocery chain denies these allegations. The fact that this profiling was still happening, and the staff was *told* to do it, caused me to relive my whole experience once again. Do you know what I did to feel better?

RAIN.

Key Points to Remember

- Discrimination is real. Black people are five times less likely to be treated with courtesy and respect than white people.

- Medical research shows that discrimination is linked to worse mental health and a number of poor physical health outcomes, including diabetes, cancer, cardiovascular disease, and inflammation.

- Deep breaths and mindfulness practices can provide the clarity you need the next time you are faced with a stressful situation with the police and others in power.

Mindfulness Practice Toolkit

Mindfulness Practice 8: Belly Breath

When you are triggered in the moment, whether it's police harassment or an offensive comment:

1 Inhale through your nose and allow your belly to expand like a balloon.

2 Exhale through your nose and allow your belly to contract toward the spine.

3 Repeat three times, or as many as needed.

Please note: You can discreetly do this exercise in front of those who are triggering you, and they don't ever have to know.

Mindfulness Practice 9: Name the Emotion

When you are feeling intense emotions, perhaps even overwhelming emotions:

1 Take a moment to observe how you are feeling.

2 Name the emotion or emotions that you are feeling.

3 Say to yourself or journal the following: "I am experiencing *[insert emotion here]*."

4 Remember that you are not your emotions and that this is temporary. This, too, shall pass.

Mindfulness Practice 10: RAIN Meditation

1 Find yourself in a comfortable seated position in a quiet place where no one will disturb you. (Put all your devices on Do Not Disturb mode.)

2 Consider playing some peaceful meditative music to relax.

3 Close your eyes and take five long, deep breaths.

4 Identify a specific instance of discrimination or racism that you have experienced.

5 Visualize the situation in detail. What is happening? Who is there? What is said or done?

6 Start with the *R* in *RAIN* and *recognize* how you are feeling. Describe it. Put words to the experience. (This step can also be a very powerful journaling exercise.)

7 The *A* in *RAIN* is for *allow*. Allow yourself to feel what you are feeling. Give yourself time to pause and be with whatever is here right now, in this moment.

8 The *I* in *RAIN* is for *investigate*. Investigate what part of your body is calling for your attention. Where in your body are you feeling heightened sensations? Perhaps it is your belly, or your shoulders, or your chest, or your neck. Describe how these sensations feel. It could be aching or sharpness or throbbing.

9 The *N* in *RAIN* is for *nurture*. Ask yourself what it might need to feel better. Perhaps you need to hear something or know something. Perhaps you need comforting words. Perhaps physical touch. Consider giving yourself a hug, or placing one hand on a sensitive area of your body. Calling on your highest self, calling on your ancestors, calling on higher powers and sources of energy that we can't see or hear, allow yourself to receive what is needed.

10 Take several deep breaths, and rest in this presence of healing.

11 When you're ready, open your eyes, and be gentle with yourself.

12 Repeat this exercise as often as needed.

CHAPTER FIVE

"You're Not Really Black"

Has anyone ever told you, either directly or indirectly, that you're not really Black? Every time I hear "I don't really consider you Black" or "You're not *Black* Black," I cringe. It gets under my skin in a way that's both irritating and painful. I want the person speaking to stop. I want the conversation to stop. I want the repetition of this experience to stop. Why? Because, either way, it ends badly. I could choose to engage, but that creates a whole lot of discomfort for both of us. It usually happens like this: I explain why I'm offended, why it's none of their business to decide just how Black I am, and I ask what they think it means to be *really* Black. They get offended because, in their mind, I just called them a racist. Choosing to engage can also be met with what is popularly known as white women's tears. These often prompt us to try to make the person feel better, even though we were the ones who were harmed in the first place.

One alternative to engaging is changing the subject. I usually do so by asking the person a benign question about themselves. People love to talk about themselves. I know it's not exactly playing a significant role in driving change, but it is self-care. Sometimes you have it in you to bear the discomfort of confronting them for the sake of the growth of humanity. Other times . . . well, you might just be exhausted.

As a child, I struggled a lot with my identity. My father is ethnically Jamaican, and Panamanian by birth. The African diaspora comes in many forms. In the case of my family, my Jamaican ancestors moved to Panama to build the Panama Canal. To the average person walking down the street in America, my father is a six-foot-one, dark-skinned Black man. My mother, on the other hand, is a tiny, barely five-foot Filipina woman who could easily pass for Hispanic. Only in the past decade did I have genetic data as a tool in this conversation about my "Blackness." Although the one-drop rule has been in effect for as long as anyone can remember, I am actually 45 percent African, including ancestors from Nigeria, Benin and Togo, Cameroon, Congo, Ivory Coast, and Ghana. And my complexion shows it. Never has anyone called me light-skinned. I usually get "brown-skinned," I suppose. If these "Blackness assessors" actually do know my heritage, perhaps their superficial assessment stems from the fact that I'm mixed or that my parents weren't born in this country?

They can say I'm not *really* Black, but I felt pretty Black when my mother cursed my hair and yanked it at the roots with a fine-tooth comb when I was a child. As she sweated and labored, attempting a task that was completely foreign to her, she made up words like *kinkinization*, which she yelled with disgust at what my father's blood had done to me. I felt so much physical pain, and I also felt a lot of self-hate. I didn't know why my hair was like this, but there was nothing I could do about it. I was born this way! I proceeded to spend decades trying to conform to a European standard of beauty, with countless relaxers and hours of blow-drying my hair straight.

I felt pretty Black in the cafeteria in high school. You know that moment when you're holding your tray, scanning the room, and trying to figure out where to sit? I don't know what high-school cafeterias look like today, but for me, at a predominately white school in the '90s, it was clear where I was welcome and where I wasn't. Of course I was welcome at the "Black table," which often was combined with the "Latin table" and the "Asian table," because . . . well, we all gotta stick together. There weren't too many of us. Toni Morrison once said, "In this country American means white. Everybody else has to hyphenate." So, I guess I sat at the "hyphenated table," and throughout it all I felt "othered." I felt excluded, like I didn't belong.

I felt pretty Black when I was harassed by the police at the grocery store for allegedly stealing deli meat after purchasing bags and bags of vegan food. When Michael Brown was shot in Ferguson, Missouri, I was dating a white man who had no patience for my reaction to what had happened. He said, "The police won't do anything to Black people *like you.*" "What do you mean, 'like me'?" I responded. Needless to say, that relationship didn't last too much longer. When I spent hours watching the police search every crevice of my car for this mystery meat, I wanted to tell him what had happened, just to show him that, regardless of what he'd meant by "like me," I, too, was subject to the degradation and harassment that Black people must endure in this country. I checked myself, though, and did not contact him. I was tired of having to prove to white people that I am, in fact, Black.

There is so much to dissect in what people mean by *"really* Black" or *"Black* Black." Clearly they have some assumptions about what being Black means. This ignorance can be exhausting, offensive, and frustrating when you're just trying to be you! We've never asked for opinions about our Blackness, and it can be challenging to figure out how to navigate a world where this happens on a regular basis.

When They Are Surprised

Have you ever gotten the "You're so articulate; how do you talk like that?" comment? Reading between the lines, we find an assumption about what Black people should sound like, and it's often associated with a lower level of education and based on media stereotypes. This comment can feel incredibly demeaning, because it already typecasts us before we even open our mouths. I have heard this comment mostly from white people; however, due to the biases in our society, I have also heard it from people of other backgrounds as well.

You might also get a surprised reaction to your interests. I constantly get comments like, "*You* play the violin?" "*You* rock climb?" I hate feeling like I'm being put in a box—as if there are certain things Black people are and aren't allowed to do. We are not a monolith. We have many interests. We come from different backgrounds. We have different experiences. We are individual souls on our own journeys. When will we be allowed to be ourselves?

Has anyone ever been surprised by your education? "*You* have a master's?" or "*You* went to Harvard?" they say incredulously. There's usually a pause while they pull themselves together. Quickly realizing their faux pas, they often follow it with a "Good for you!" This condescending comment really stings! Even in a world where we had a Black president who went to Harvard Law, people are surprised.

One of my friends from college loves to start sentences with "As a Harvard economist . . ." just because she knows it will shock people; they typically respond with wide-eyed disbelief. We have come to expect this reaction so often that it's just comical for us. Making light of it with jokes is one form of healing, but it doesn't last for more than a moment.

When you get a surprised reaction to your interests, experience, and education, it can often feel like a reminder of where we were born in the hierarchy of America. Sometimes it might ignite a fire in you to continue surprising them, so that one day they won't be shocked by a Black person's accomplishments or interests. Until that day comes, we can take these opportunities to practice calming our nervous system when we are annoyed, frustrated, and, sometimes, sad.

When you hear these comments, you can always resort to the practice I shared regarding police interactions in chapter 4: the Belly Breath.

Without them, your reflexive reaction to "*You* have a master's?" or "*You* do [*insert almost anything here*]?" might be to get angry and say something really cutting in response. You might want to curse them out. You might want to go on a long tirade about stereotypes and their role in perpetuating them. But the Belly Breath keeps the peace. Breathe in through the belly with intention, really expanding the belly like you mean it. Exhale with intention, using your abdominal muscles to pull your belly back in. Even just one of these breaths gives you enough time to pause and decide what you want to say with intention, versus a reflexive reaction. You still might tell them about stereotypes, but perhaps with a tone that doesn't scream "F*** You!" so your message lands in a place where the other person can receive and learn from it.

When They Tell You about You

Although experiencing white people's surprise about you hurts, at least it is posed in the form of a question, which implies a small willingness to learn. It is much worse when statements are made unapologetically, as if they are fact. Stereotypes about what we are supposed to be like and how we are supposed to act can be extremely harmful. Rooted in this country's history of slavery, segregation, and systemic racism, these stereotypes can make us feel like we are "less than," which can impact not only our self-esteem but also our ability to access opportunities across all aspects of our lives. Whether we are at the car dealership or trying to get a mortgage at the bank, we are treated differently, and this disparate treatment has a direct impact on our quality of life. Moreover, it can be extremely tiring to feel like you are constantly on the defensive, trying to prove people wrong.

When statements promoting stereotypes are made in the workplace, it is even more challenging because our reactions can have an impact on our employment and therefore our ability to eat and live. At one of the companies where I worked, a white person said to a Black colleague, "You're probably a single mother, right?" As you might imagine, this was not well received. First of all, even if the colleague were a single mother, it was really none of this person's business. Second of all, what made her assume this? (Obviously this is a rhetorical question.)

At the same company, following a disagreement between a Black colleague and a white one, the white supervisor said, to console her white team member, "You know how they can get." Imagine if you were the Black person in this situation, or any Black person within hearing distance. You now know that the supervisor thinks that all Black people act a certain way, so it doesn't matter what you are like as an individual. You already have a label. And, in this case, I'm sure it reeks of the "angry Black woman" stereotype.

In situations like these, you might want to let them have it. You might want to get mad, get all up in their face, and tell them what you really think. But it's a job, and your paycheck is real. So, what can you do?

In addition to the Belly Breath, an extra-long exhalation can have a similar effect on the nervous system. The next time someone says something offensive to you, give it a try. With intention, let your exhalation be as slow and long as you can, and see how you feel. Every time I take an extra-long exhalation, my shoulders sink back down and I can feel myself relax. From this place of calm, you can decide how to respond in a way that allows you to keep your job, and, if you do decide to leave, you can do so on your own terms.

When They Assume You Were Born and Raised in Africa

Although stereotypes exist regarding our mannerisms, our socio-economic class, and our education levels, confronting the ignorant assumption that *Black* automatically means culturally and geographically African is when I have most needed this extra-long exhalation for my own well-being.

A couple years ago I performed at a small outdoor concert, and after my set a white woman approached me and said, "I really loved the show! You know, I had a roommate from Africa once."

In a split second, my mind had already gone through a rant of *Not again! Why is she thinking this is relevant, right now? Does she think that because I'm Black, I'm from Africa? Does she think that perhaps I might know her African roommate? Is she trying to tell me that she is "woke" because she lived with an African once? Was this her attempt to put a fist in the air and say "Black power" in solidarity? She was clearly trying to connect, but . . . really?*

Comments like these are frustrating because they blatantly ignore the critical history that led Black people to be on this continent in the first place. Although we might be of African descent, the slave trade led to the mass dispersion of our people around the globe. To assume that we were born and raised in Africa is a direct dismissal of this history. This ignorance suggests a belief that our history is not worth anyone's time to learn about, and a very understandable reaction might be to get triggered.

Rather than respond immediately to this woman's comment, I took an extra-long exhalation. All that wound up inside of me during that split-second rant was able to loosen up. The muscles in my forehead, which had scrunched up almost immediately in reaction to what she said, began to relax. My shoulders lowered, my back straightened, and I held my head high and responded, "That's interesting; what country in Africa?"

Dumbfounded, as if I had really given her the hardest *Jeopardy!* question in history, she looked confused, paused, and said, "Oh, I have no idea. I guess I never asked!"

"Well, Africa is a big continent," I explained. "I've climbed Kilimanjaro in Tanzania, and I built houses with Habitat for Humanity in Ethiopia, but that's the extent of my Africa travels. Did you think I was from Africa also?"

"Ummm . . . well . . . I mean . . . ," she stuttered with an embarrassed smile.

"Well, the African diaspora is very expansive. My family is from Jamaica, Panama, and the Philippines." And, with that, I figured my work on the education front for that day was sufficient. I excused myself from the conversation and went to seek out a Black friend at the gathering for refuge. "Can you believe she said that?" I asked my friend.

"Yes, girl, I can," she responded, shaking her head.

When They Say They "Don't See Color"

When referring to race, has anyone ever told you that they're "colorblind"? *Blindness* typically means that you are not *able* to see. However, in this case, it is a choice. They are *choosing* not to see skin color, and in doing so they are choosing not to see both the inequities that continue to exist because of race and the impact on our community. Dismissing our experiences as Black people in America, they are ignoring our history and further justifying the current system as they enjoy their privilege in society.

A white coworker once told me, "I see you as colorless. When I see you, I don't see color," as if ignoring my Blackness were a compliment. Every time I look in the mirror, I see a beautiful brown complexion—that definitely looks like color to me.

To the white woman who called me "colorless" at work, although I understand that you probably had the best intentions, I have a song I'd like to share with you:

"Say It Loud—I'm Black and I'm Proud"

—James Brown

Although people act like being Black is a stain on our existence, a trait that they choose not to see in their attempt to be a good person, being Black is not an inherently negative thing. I love being Black and I will define what being Black is for myself. I will not hide it. (I physically cannot hide it.) Nor will I, or any other Black person, pretend to be colorless to fit into a mold created by white people. Our color is part of who we are, it's a part of our culture, it's a part of what makes us *us*.

In a 1982 speech at Harvard University, Audre Lorde said, "If I didn't define myself, I would be crunched into other people's fantasies for me and eaten alive." We must have agency in how we define ourselves. Every time someone tries to put you into a box, I invite you to take a moment to reflect on what being Black means to you. Turn off your computer and your phone. Close your eyes. Place a hand on your heart and take five deep breaths to establish your center and to anchor yourself in your truth. With each breath, allow yourself to release any heightened emotions that the comment might have stirred up. Allow the hand on your heart to offer you a sense of comfort and a sense of safety. After the fifth breath, ask yourself the question, "What does it mean to be Black?"

What's coming up for you? Sit with it for a few minutes, and when you're ready, write it down in your journal. Notice how whatever you wrote makes you feel.

After the "colorless" comment, this is what came up for me:

To be Black is to have incredible strength regardless of the direction the wind blows. To be Black is to be resilient. We get back up when we get knocked down. We find a way to keep on going in any way that we can. To be Black is to be persistent and to fight for what we know is right. To be Black is to be versatile in our skills and to be able to adapt to whatever our circumstances require. We are basically superheroes in my mind. We have been and continue to be tested, and we are still here. To be Black is to be a trailblazer. There are so many of us that have been the "first" in whatever it is we are pursuing. To be the first takes courage, it takes determination, and it takes grit. In fact, we were the first of the species, since the first humans emerged in Africa! To be Black is to have independence in thought, to challenge the status quo. To be Black is to have flavor, in our art, in our music, in our writing, in our fashion, and in all things. To be Black is to be creative. To be Black is to live with love.

When I felt like I was finished, at least for that particular moment, I opened my eyes and smiled with so much pride. How good it felt to be alive. How good it felt to be in this Black body, carrying with me the wisdom and the superpowers of all who came before me.

When Their Negativity about Blackness Starts to Wear You Down

When the negative comments about Black people start to wear you down, I invite you to sit down and make a list of the Black people who you admire most. Who would be on your list? As you write down every name, pause and think about why you're adding them. This, too, is mindfulness. Rather than robotically accepting the stereotypes and negativity, mindfully pay attention to the truth that already sits inside you, and how that truth makes you feel.

Every time I make a list like this, there are more people whom I want to add. Dr. Harriett Jenkins is always first on the list. When I was twelve years old, she was in her mid-sixties, and she took me in and became my hero and my mentor. She was responsible for so many of my firsts—symphonies, plays, ballets, operas. She shared stories of her life, from spending almost twenty years creating equal-opportunity programs at NASA to desegregating schools in the Berkeley Unified School District in California. She always gave it to me straight and asked me the hard questions.

Kim Keating was my manager at my very first internship, the summer before I went to college. She was a trailblazer who left Little Rock, Arkansas, and she was the first Black person I ever met who had gone to Harvard Business School. She made me believe that I could do and be anything.

My Auntie Marcia was my first exposure to an independent Black woman. She showed me that marriage and children do not define a woman's self-worth.

Mr. Meeks was my first Black violin teacher. At the age of eighty, he taught me that the violin is also for us, and "don't let anyone ever tell you different!"

Linda Smith gave me violin lessons in her tiny studio apartment in D.C., and she taught me that it's not about the money but about love for the music.

Ashanti Decker was my roommate in college, who demonstrated so much bravery in being unapologetic about her sexuality, despite the disapproval of her very religious parents.

My friend Simret's mother was a matriarch, successful business-woman, and pillar of the community. When Simret passed away at age thirty-seven, she showed me that we can channel our inner strength when we suffer an incredible loss.

When I was in culture shock after having just moved to the whitest place I had ever lived, Denver, Colorado, my friend Narkita showed me that community can be found and created, as her *Black in Denver* portrait and interview series grew from just an idea to an exhibit in the Museum of Contemporary Art to a community of awe-inspiring folks. In fact, everyone she featured should also be on this list!

Although I could go on about the people in my personal life who have had a huge impact on me, there are so many Black heroes who have shaped me.

- Spring Washam—cofounder of the East Bay Meditation Center

- Jan Willis—joined a Tibetan monastery instead of the Black Panther Party

- Resmaa Menakem—Somatic Abolitionism

- Ruth King, founder of the Mindful of Race Institute

- adrienne maree brown, author of *Pleasure Activism* and *Emergent Strategy*

- Tricia Hersey, founder of the Nap Ministry—"Rest is Resistance"

Black writers whom I have immense gratitude for:

- Maya Angelou, James Baldwin, Audre Lorde, Toni Morrison, Alice Walker, Zora Neale Hurston, Lorraine Hansberry, Octavia Butler, Sara Lawrence-Lightfoot

- Poet Amanda Gorman—the next generation bringing it in full force!

Those who fought for change and risked their lives in the process:

- Harriet Tubman, Frederick Douglass, Marcus Garvey, Dr. Martin Luther King Jr., Malcolm X, the Little Rock Nine

- Nelson Mandela—taught me about resilience, about peace, and about justice

Those who were wrongfully imprisoned due to systemic racism:

- Assata Shakur, former Black Liberation Army member, convicted of murder with zero evidence and a number of unjust proceedings in the trial

- Colin Warner, a Brooklyn man who was eventually freed after twenty-one years in prison for a wrongful conviction

Those who created magic with music:

- Marian Anderson, Duke Ellington, Louis Armstrong, Miles Davis, John Coltrane, Billie Holiday, Bessie Smith, Josephine Baker, Nina Simone, Stevie Wonder, Prince, Michael Jackson, Whitney Houston

Black artists—their art, their soul, and their unique messages inspire me to let my own voice sing:

- Painters Jacob Lawrence and Jean-Michel Basquiat, Harlem Renaissance sculptors like Augusta Savage, dance icons like Alvin Ailey

Media and entertainment:

- Cicely Tyson, Pam Grier, Halle Berry, Kerry Washington, Ava DuVernay, RuPaul

- Oprah—she is and always will be such a force!

Those who made game-changing contributions to science and technology:

- George Washington Carver; NASA mathematicians and engineers Katherine Johnson, Dorothy Vaughan, and Mary Jackson; Walt Braithwaite, who developed computer-aided design (CAD) systems for Boeing, which are used everywhere today; Gladys West, whose modeling work was the basis of GPS (Every time I use Google Maps, I give thanks to her!); astrophysicist Neil deGrasse Tyson, who is constantly dropping knowledge; Kimberly Bryant, founder of Black Girls Code, because she is laying the foundation for what future Black inventors and engineers will create!

Those with the courage, willpower, and skills to be "the first":

- Alexa Canady, the first Black woman neurosurgeon in the United States; Mae Jemison, the first Black woman to travel into space; Ursula Burns, the first Black female CEO of a Fortune 500 company

- Barack Obama and Michelle Obama. When Obama was elected, I cried tears of joy. I never thought that day would come. And then it did.

Every time I make my list, I am beaming with both pride and hope. These amazing human beings define what Black is to me. These amazing human beings make me believe that my skin color is an asset, not a flaw, no matter what anyone has to say about it.

"Say it loud—I'm Black and I'm proud!"

Key Points to Remember

· You have the power to define what being Black means to you. Remember the words of Audre Lorde: "If I didn't define myself, I would be crunched into other people's fantasies for me and eaten alive."

· When someone questions your Blackness, be mindful of self-care in deciding whether and how to engage with their comments. Check in with yourself and do what feels right for you at that moment.

· The Belly Breath is applicable in a number of situations, from remaining calm when faced with the police to dealing with white people trying to tell you what you should or shouldn't be like, based on your skin color.

Mindfulness Practice Toolkit

Mindfulness Practice 11: Extra-Long Exhalation

When someone says something offensive and irritating about being Black, before you respond:

1 Exhale through your nose as slowly and for as long as possible.

2 Consider slowly counting to three during the exhalation (e.g., "One Mississippi, two Mississippi, three Mississippi").

3 Inhale like you normally would.

4 Again exhale as slowly as you can for as long as you can.

5 Repeat as many times as needed.

Mindfulness Practice 12:
Heart-Centered: What Does Being Black Mean to You?
When all the negative stereotypes about Black people start to wear
you down:

1 Find yourself in a quiet place where no one will disturb you.
(Put all your devices on Do Not Disturb mode.)

2 Close your eyes.

3 Place one hand on your heart.

4 Take five deep, long breaths.

5 After the fifth breath, ask yourself the question, "What does it
mean to be Black?"

6 Sit for a few minutes and receive whatever comes up for you.

7 Write it down in your journal.

8 Notice how whatever comes up makes you feel.

Mindfulness Practice 13: Black People You Admire Most
When you need a reminder about how amazing Black people really are:

1 Get a piece of paper (or open a document on your computer) and
make a list of Black people whom you admire.

2 Write down whoever comes to mind, in any order. Include people
whom you know personally, and people whom you don't. Include
people who are alive and people who are no longer with us.

3 As you write down each name, pause and think about why you are
putting this person on the list.

4 When you're finished with your list, take a moment to read every
name on it. As you do so, notice how this list makes you feel.

CHAPTER SIX

"That's Not My Name!"

"*I am* not *Laurence Fishburne,*" Samuel L. Jackson told a news anchor on live TV when he was mistakenly asked about a Superbowl commercial that Laurence Fishburne had starred in. "We don't all look alike!" he exclaimed.

I feel him. During Thanksgiving dinner at a friend's house, an older white doctor asked me in all seriousness whether I was Samuel L. Jackson's daughter. While Zoe Jackson and I both have names that start with the letter *Z*, that's about all we have in common—except that we are both Black women in America and therefore, apparently, interchangeable. I was so stunned, I didn't know what to say. Initially confused and then appalled, I responded, "Ummm . . . no, I am not." Sadly, this is not the first time I've been called the wrong name by a white person. Although this was the first time I was confused for Samuel L. Jackson's daughter!

The more typical name confusion happens to me at work. Although I'm often the only Black person in the room, on the floor, or in the building, in the rare cases where there is another Black woman at the company, my white colleagues will call me by that person's name, and vice versa. Has this ever happened to you?

This awkward moment, especially when it's in a group setting, is the worst. I was in a meeting once and someone called me Tiana, the name of a Black coworker. Upon first hearing the name, there was a quick moment of confusion in my mind. *Tiana? Oh . . . they're doing it again.* When I realized that I had just been confused with another Black woman, I felt this almost electric shock of annoyance. Do you know this feeling? For me, it's like my shoulders and my stomach tighten, and I can't even pay attention to what's going on because all I can think of is, *What? Tiana? That's not my f—ing name!*

At this point, you're faced with the question of how to respond. Do you ignore it and let it slide? Or do you let it all out? It's easy for your emotional triggers to dominate how you react. It can be such a complex and deep-rooted array of feelings. *They don't see me. They don't respect me. They don't value me.* Whether it's anger or frustration or annoyance, all these emotions can come out in your tone, and we all know the potential consequences of that. So, what should you do?

When People Confuse You with Another Black Person

There is no right or wrong way to deal with this situation, but what I will tell you is that you're better off responding after your nervous system has had a chance to calm down. Remember the Belly Breath? This same technique can be used here and any time you are triggered. From this calmer place, you will identify the right thing for you in that moment. When I heard my coworker say, "Tiana, will you take that one?" I did a Belly Breath. Just that one second of a deep breath allowed me to respond from a place that wouldn't get me labeled an "angry Black woman."

"Actually, it's Zee. But, sure, I'd be happy to," I said, with a fake smile that would get me through the interaction. I'm not recommending that you respond the way I did, nor am I saying that you should use a fake smile. Instead I invite you to try this Belly Breath in the moment so that you can respond from your highest self, so that however you react will be something that you can stand by. We are all different, and you know what's best for you. This breath allows you to channel that and act accordingly.

When People Mispronounce Your Name

Mustering up the courage to correct people about my name has been a long journey that started in my childhood. If you have a name that is outside the "norm," you might also remember the feeling of dread on the first day of school. It's time for roll call, and they are going down the list. You know your name is coming up soon, and you're holding your breath, squeezing the seat of your chair, dreading the moment that you know is going to come at any second—the complete butchering of the pronunciation of your name.

My parents named me Zhalisa, pronounced "Cha-leesa." I recognize that this is not intuitive, so I don't judge anyone for not getting it right the first time. However, it's everything else that comes with this interaction that has been exhausting. It starts with the excruciating pause, which I experienced the first time I ever set foot in a school, at age four. The teacher goes down the student roster with a certain rhythm. "Jennifer?" "Here." "Michael?" "Here." "Sarah?" "Here." And then the moment arrives. Awkward pause. Perplexed look on the teacher's face, followed by "Za-ha-ly-za?"

The sound of someone butchering your name can feel like fingernails scraping a chalkboard. You feel it under your skin. It gets to you in a way that you feel all throughout your body, and it doesn't exactly feel good. When I was four years old, on that first day of school, I corrected

my teacher and told her how to say my name. She laughed and said, "Well, I am never going to be able to get that right," with a disparaging *You people* sort of tone. I felt ashamed that my name was different from everyone else's, that I was in some sort of "other" category. I felt like I was a burden to my teacher. I felt judged for something I had nothing to do with. I didn't name myself! And I was angry at my parents for giving me a name that caused this situation in the first place!

When it's an authority figure, like a teacher, it is so much harder to find the confidence to correct them. As a child, it's easy to feel intimidated, and often teachers gaslight students into thinking it's not a big deal, forcing them to just accept the mispronunciation. I have friends who gave up on correcting their teachers, accepting the fact that, at school, they would just have a different name.

The first time someone says your name wrong, it might be forgivable. However, it feels so much worse when you're constantly having to correct them, especially at work. It's like they aren't even trying, which makes you feel like you are less important, less valuable, and not worth their time. If people can learn how to say Schwarzenegger, Tchaikovsky, and Dostoyevsky, why can't they take the time to learn your name?

I have been explaining my name for as long as I can remember. I was wondering just how much of my life has been spent on this task, so I did some quick math. I would say this happens three times a week, it usually takes five minutes per explanation, and I've been explaining since I was about four years old (so, for thirty-seven years at this writing). That comes to 28,860 minutes of my life. I wonder what new skill I could have gained instead during this time. Alas, I will never know.

Every time my name is mispronounced I ask myself whether it's worth it to correct them. Thoughts like *It will make them uncomfortable* or *I don't want to be a burden* come up. However, there's a phrase that I repeat to myself whenever I'm in this situation:

Today, I choose me.

This simple phrase reminds me that it's not about anyone else's comfort. It reminds me that I deserve to be treated with respect, and I deserve to be called by my name. If you're debating whether you should prioritize someone else's comfort over your own, I invite you to repeat this to yourself five times:

Today, I choose me.
Today, I choose me.
Today, I choose me.
Today, I choose me.
Today, I choose me.

Now ask yourself what you should do. Your answer will be very clear.

When People Decide Your Name for You

Have you ever been in a situation where, rather than try to pronounce your name, people decide to just call you something else? When I was in fifth grade, my white classmates didn't like my name, so do you know what they called me?

Chelsea.

I didn't even like the name Chelsea, but did I have a choice? Nope. At that time, Bill Clinton was president and Chelsea Clinton was also in Washington, D.C., at a local private school. I have nothing against Chelsea Clinton, and she's done a lot in her adult years, but when we were in elementary school I wanted nothing to do with her.

As an adult, I have heard this a lot: "Can I just call you Lisa?" We all have things that trigger us, that get under our skin. For me, this is one of them. It reminds me of the scene in Alex Haley's *Roots*, where the character Kunta Kinte is repeatedly whipped for not accepting the name Toby, which his slaveowners imposed on him. Although people might make the point that so much progress has been made because at least I was "asked" if it was okay to change my name, it often feels like a rhetorical question, where they barely wait for a response and just assume that this is acceptable.

When someone asks me if they can call me Lisa, this is my internal rant:

Can you call me Lisa? Did I say my name was Lisa? *What gives you the right to rename me? You are not my master. This world is not here to be convenient for you! No, you may* not *call me Lisa. I can't believe you have the audacity to even ask that!*

A recent meme coined the term *caucacity*—the audacity of Caucasians. This caucacity makes my blood boil. If it were a one-time incident, perhaps it would feel less charged, but it is hours and hours of my life!

Have you ever wondered what you can do to manage this anger? How can you calm yourself and cool off when you're so annoyed at the constant caucacity we must endure? If you're this far along in the book, you will guess what I'm going to say: Breathe. Another breathing technique I learned in India is the Cooling Breath[*]. Whenever you're emotionally overheated, find yourself a quiet place, close your eyes, and try this.

Stick out your tongue and roll it, curling the outer edges toward the center to form an almost tubelike shape. Slowly inhale through your rolled tongue, and feel the coolness of the air entering your entire system. After a long, slow inhalation, let out a long, slow exhalation through your nose. Inhale once more through your rolled tongue and exhale through your nose as you listen to the sound of your breath mimicking that of ocean waves slowly coming in, slowly going out. Allow the coolness to spread throughout your body, and relax. Take ten to fifteen deep breaths like this and immediately feel yourself grow calmer. If you can't roll your tongue or if it feels like too much effort, you can do a similar version of this exercise without it. Instead, bring your lips to a very teeth-exposing smile, and breathe in through closed teeth, and exhale through your nose. You get the same effects, but it's a little less

---

[*] This practice is based on the traditional *pranayama* called *Sheetali* and *Sheetkari*.

Cooling Breath

Option A: Tongue Roll

Inhale through the mouth

Exhale through the nose

Option B: Teeth Smile

Inhale through the mouth

Exhale through the nose

awkward for the tongue, which I sometimes find hard to keep in that rolled position for so many breaths.

In addition to cooling the mind and the body, this technique is amazing for reducing inflammation; calming inflammatory skin conditions like eczema, which I struggled with for many years; alleviating excess hunger and thirst; and so much more. I have found that this cooling state of calm after name butchering is a much better place from which to really take back the power around my name.

During slavery, we were robbed of our surnames. That's how I ended up with the last name Clarke, the name of a slave owner. However, first names have historically been a way of passing on Black culture. For example, "in the 1920 census, 99% of all men with the first name of Booker were black, as were 80% of all men named Perlie or its variations." These were almost exclusively Black names and there was a sense of pride in that. In the '60s and '70s, the Black Power movement inspired an increase in new names as empowerment and expression. We find meaning and inspiration in our names. There are more than 580 million girls with the name Aaliyah, which means "to ascend." It also means "high" and "sublime." Barack Hussein Obama's name has a powerful meaning as well. Barack means "blessed" and Hussein means "good" or "beautiful." Cassius Clay changed his name to Muhammad Ali as a reflection of his spiritual path with the Nation of Islam.

Naming is our right and our power to define ourselves and our legacy as we choose. In her baby-naming book, *Proud Heritage*, author Elza Dinwiddie-Boyd shares that creative naming "is largely and profoundly the legacy of African-Americans." *Freakonomics* authors Steven Levitt and Stephen Dubner explain that "nearly 30 percent of the black girls are given a name that is unique among the names of every baby, white and black, born . . . in California."

A few years ago, I decided to reclaim my right to choose my own name. The name I was given didn't have any specific historical or cultural significance in my family or my heritage. My brother made it up, and my father made up the spelling. However, I felt like my name was associated with the person that my parents had wanted me to be. I grew up in a very strict household, and my path was outlined in great detail. They chose my classes in school, and they chose my extracurricular activities. They tried to choose my major in college. They even tried to choose my friends, though I just lied and made friends with whomever I wanted. When I was a child, they also informed me of their choice for my husband. Clearly that didn't happen.

Close friends had been calling me Zee for years. The people who called me Zee were those who loved me unconditionally. The people who called me Zee were referring to a person who was bold and creative, a person who was wild and free, a person who, I realized, was the true me. So, when I decided to lead with "My name is Zee," this was me having agency about not only my name, but my identity and my life. This was me defining me, for myself. But it wasn't an easy journey to build up the confidence to use my own voice in this way. I was a shy child who did what she was told, and our childhood personas tend to stick with us.

A breathwork technique called the Lion's Breath[*] is really helpful in finding your voice and building up your confidence. On the first day of a new job, when I knew I was going to have to correct so many people about how to pronounce my name, I did this practice in the bathroom before interacting with any of my new colleagues. When I was working up the courage to inform everyone that my new name was Zee, I did this practice every morning in the mirror.

I know it looks weird, and my version looks even more animalistic than the traditional version, so I encourage you to always do it in private. If you need an instant boost in confidence, so that you can find the courage to speak up about your name, or anything else that's bothering you, I invite you to try this.

Find a private place, ideally with a mirror. (Note that bathrooms work great for this.) Bend your arms at ninety-degree angles, to resemble a goalpost. With your hands up, palms facing forward, and fingers outstretched like the "jazz hands" of the '80s, inhale deeply through your nose. As you exhale, stick your tongue out as far as

---

[*] This practice is inspired by a hatha yoga pose called *Simhasana* in Sanskrit.

Lion's Breath

Inhale through your nose

On a slow, long exhalation,
stick your tongue out

possible and make a forceful hissing sound in your throat. Inhale once again through your nose, and when you exhale stick your tongue out and down toward your chin as far as it will go, while making this very animal-like sound with your breath. Repeat this for three to five breaths, contorting your facial muscles and widening your eyes, really expressing the sound with your face. Try it and see how you feel!

Doing this makes me feel wild and uninhibited. I feel a raw energy surge from inside me, breaking through any of the rules that I had been taught to follow. I feel energized, like this is my time to spread my wings and fly! How does it make you feel?

When I was in India, I learned that the Lion's Breath opens up the throat chakra. The chakra system is a network of energy channels in the body, first defined in India between 1500 and 500 BC. The throat chakra, so named because of its location in the body, is the center of communication, self-expression, and our ability to speak our personal truth. Activating our throat chakra with the Lion's Breath helps to boost our confidence. It is also said to help our circulation and reduce tension, and my favorite benefit of the Lion's Breath is its anti-aging effect! We all know that Black don't crack, but it doesn't hurt to give that a little assistance because . . . well, why not?

On my first day at a new job, because I had done my Lion's Breath that morning, I was prepared. I was ready with a kind yet assertive correction of their pronunciation when I was called "Za-ha-ly-za." I was ready when I got the confused and judgmental "Hmmm . . . how did your parents come up with that?" The lioness inside me was ready to roar in all her glory.

When I moved to a new city and started introducing myself as Zee, the Lion's Breath gave me the voice to say it with pride. I was introducing the me that I was choosing to be. The me that was free.

"My name is Zee Clarke. What's your name?"

Key Points to Remember

- When you are triggered by someone calling you the wrong name or repeatedly mispronouncing your name, practice a breathing technique like the Belly Breath or an extra-long exhalation to calm your nervous system and respond from a less reactive headspace.

- If people can learn how to say Schwarzenegger, Tchaikovsky, and Dostoyevsky, they can take the time to learn your name. Period.

- Naming is our right and our power to define ourselves as we choose. Use your voice, and don't let anyone take that power away from you. It is yours, and it will always be yours.

Mindfulness Practice Toolkit

Mindfulness Practice 14: Today, I Choose Me

If you're debating whether you should correct someone who is butchering your name and you are considering prioritizing their comfort over your own:

1 Close your eyes.

2 Take a deep breath.

3 Repeat this phrase five times aloud: "Today, I choose me."

4 With each repetition, say it louder and with more confidence.

5 Take a moment to pause and listen to your inner guidance about what the right course of action is for you.

Mindfulness Practice 15: Cooling Breath[*]
When your blood is boiling and you are so angry at what you have just experienced:

1 Find yourself a quiet place and close your eyes.

2 Choose the best option for you:

Option A: Tongue Roll. Stick out your tongue and roll it by curling the outer edges toward the center, forming an almost tubelike shape.

Option B: Teeth Smile. Bring your lips to a smile that exposes your teeth. Ensure that the top and bottom teeth are touching.

3 Inhale slowly through either your rolled tongue or your teeth. Feel the cool air enter your body.

4 Exhale slowly through your nose. Feel the air leave your body and notice the effects on areas of your body that were tight.

5 Repeat for ten to fifteen breaths.

Mindfulness Practice 16: Lion's Breath[**]
When you need to build the confidence to allow your true voice to shine, whether it's correcting someone about your name or forcing others to really see you:

1 Bend your elbows and bring your arms to a ninety-degree angle, forming a goalpost with your arms, palms straight up and facing forward, fingers stretched wide.

2 Inhale deeply through your nose.

3 As you exhale, stick your tongue out as far as possible and make a forceful hissing sound in your throat. Allow the exhalation to be as long and slow as possible.

4 Let your face fully express the sound, allowing your eyes to grow wide and your facial muscles to fully engage.

5 Repeat for three breaths.

[*] Cooling Breath should not be practiced if you have the following: low blood pressure, chronic constipation, asthma, a cough or cold, or congestion.
[**] Lion's Breath should not be practiced if you have a recent or chronic injury to your face, neck, or tongue.

105

CHAPTER SEVEN

The Only

Have you ever looked around and realized that you were the only Black person in the room? Perhaps you were the only person of color. Perhaps you were also the only woman. This has been my life since the third grade. In elementary school I was usually the only Black person in my year. In high school I was usually the only Black person in my honors and AP classes. This was the case at music camp and ballet. This continues to be the case in my adulthood. Whether I am snowboarding, rock climbing, or in a work meeting, I am usually the only Black person present. As I rose through the ranks professionally, I realized that I was also the only Black person or Black woman in leadership wherever I worked, especially in the tech industry.

I asked a mentor of mine what it felt like for her to be "the only" in her career, and she responded, "That's like asking Black people during segregation what it felt like to sit at the back of the bus. . . . It just is what it is! It's been my normal since as long as I can remember. A better question is, What would it feel like to *not* be 'the only'?"

I Walked Alone

I didn't let myself feel it.
Numb to a reality that was my norm,
I walked alone.

Driven by the knowing that this was my shot,
and that failure was not an option,
I walked alone.

Feeling the intensity of their gaze,
I knew that every misstep would be watched and noticed.
I walked alone.

Yearning for another set of eyes like mine,
yearning for a sense of understanding and community,
I walked alone.

Sleepless nights of anxiety-filled spirals,
the pressure of perfection overwhelming,
I walked alone.

Reminding myself of our trailblazer ancestors,
those who were the firsts of their time,
I walked alone.

Grateful for the opportunity to create paths for our children,
grateful for the fire inside of me still burning,
I walked alone.

Knowing that this was temporary,
knowing that one day the world would look different,
I walked alone.

The first thing that comes to mind for me is that I would feel less lonely. Being the only Black woman—and often Black person or woman, period—can feel so isolating. I attended an implicit-bias training at work once, and all I wanted was to see another Black person in the room so we could look at each other, and perhaps do a joint eye roll, acknowledging how much this training had missed the mark. The facilitator was trying to demonstrate that we all make associations and assumptions based on the identity of others. She had great intentions. However, the exercise and example she gave was that of herself. She said, "I am a German woman, I am forty-five years old, and I live in an upper-middle-class suburb. What can you assume about me based on this?" The responses included the stereotypes that she is organized and financially responsible because she is German and that she is affluent based on her neighborhood. Some participants shared thoughts about what her career might be assumed to be—technical roles like accounting or engineering. The takeaway was supposed to be that we all make assumptions, and she left it at that.

I couldn't help but think to myself, *How are the mostly positive stereotypes about her being German supposed to teach white people that the typically negative stereotypes that they believe about Black people have a massive impact on the state of Black people in America today? How will this change Black people's ability to get hired and promoted at this company? And why am I, a Black person who already has extensive firsthand experience of being stereotyped, required to take this training?* If another Black person were in the room, I would have immediately given them a look. They would have looked back at me, and we would have shared a very silent, but comforting, moment suggesting that we were both equally bothered by what was happening. But, alas, there was no one there but me. Instead this group of white people nodded as if they had had some profound realizations, and the training continued as if we were all better for having attended.

In situations like this, you might question your reactions because you're the only one that seems to notice or care. At first, I was surprised that *this* was the example used to teach about biases. Then I was just insulted. There was very little mention of Black, Latinx, Asian, or Indigenous communities during the entire two hours. Instead it was just an implied comparison, and I was left alone to shake my head. In these moments, count on your community outside of work as a source of comfort and validation. A simple phone call or text message from someone who understands can be life-changing. For me, my family members and friends are my lifeline. They help me recognize that they would have reacted the same way.

When you feel like "the only," it's important to rely on those in your support system to validate you. Be sure to call on them whenever necessary. Because, though you may be alone at work, you are not alone in life.

The Pressure to Perform

In addition to loneliness, being the only Black person or person of color at work can carry an intense pressure to be flawless in your performance. We all know that we have to be twice as good as any white person just to get the same amount of respect, to get comparable promotions and compensation, and to be treated equally. It can feel like you're being watched through a lens that has a much broader perspective than just your own performance. It can feel like every move you make represents the capabilities of your entire race. It can feel like, if you mess up, they will never hire another person of color again.

Several years ago, I took a role in enterprise sales, having never worked in sales in my life. I was the only Black woman out of more than 500 employees, and the pressure was on. If you've never worked in sales before, there is one word that is motivating for some and haunting for others—*quotas*. Everything that you sell is measured, not just against your own quota but against your peers'. In addition, your sales numbers are visible to everyone on your team. Although one might say that this is the most objective way to measure performance, there are so many additional layers to this for a Black woman, and as the only Black woman at the company.

First of all, there were a ton of inbound leads, companies reaching out to the firm expressing interest. The head of sales would very subjectively decide who got which ones. Some leads were very attractive: large companies with deep pockets and a readiness to spend. These leads were gold. If you hooked a big whale, you could go from 0 to 30 percent of your quota with just that one deal. On the other hand, some of the leads were duds, a waste of time from a salesperson's perspective. These leads came in many forms: Sometimes it was clear from the beginning that what they were asking for just wasn't what we offered; sometimes the person contacting us just didn't have the budget; sometimes the company was so small that there was no way they could afford us.

I couldn't help but wonder whether I was getting equal treatment to the white men on my team regarding the leads we got. They could bond with the head of sales, who was also a white man, about things like sports, cars, and the latest gadgets on the market. I felt like I had to work so much harder to be liked, because it would have a direct impact on my compensation and my job security. I would see some of my white male colleagues land these epic deals, and I would wonder if I had been set up for failure from the beginning.

If someone has an off quarter or an off year, the decision to fire them can be quick and heartless. I couldn't afford to be on the chopping block. I didn't have a ton of savings. Unlike many of my white friends, I didn't have wealthy parents to pay my rent if something were to happen. If I were fired for not meeting my numbers, I felt like my self-esteem would be crushed to such an extent that I wouldn't be able to get up again. Not only that: As my colleagues looked at the team's sales chart, I felt like the question subconsciously (or consciously) in their head would be, *How's the Black woman performing?* They hadn't had a Black woman in this role before, and I needed them to know that they hadn't made a mistake in hiring me. I felt like all this was on my shoulders.

Feeling like there was no room for error, I gave it my all. I read all the books about best practices in sales. I sought out friends who had experience in the field. I became an aggressive hunter in my outbound sales strategy, because if I wasn't going to receive the good inbound leads, I would have to make my own.

Yet the anxiety from all the pressure was too much to handle. My stomach was in a gut-wrenching knot so regularly that it started to feel like the norm. I couldn't sleep. I would wake up in the middle of the night, wondering if this deal or that deal would close. I would stay up for hours, worried, because though my white colleagues might be given the latitude of just having a "bad day," I might be deemed "not a good fit" for the organization. If you can relate to this experience, you should know that you are not alone. Anxiety is real, and long-term anxiety can be detrimental to our health, causing depression, digestive problems, insomnia, chronic pain, substance-abuse disorders, suicidal thoughts, and . . . the list goes on.

When you feel overwhelmed by anxiety or have trouble sleeping, I invite you to try a breathing technique that has helped me in these intense moments. It's called 4-7-8 Breathing, and it is a powerful tool for helping you find a sense of calm, because it stimulates your parasympathetic nervous system. It helps lower your blood pressure, reduce anxiety, and ease your body into sleep.

Make sure that your back is straight, so that you can take advantage of your full lung capacity. Inhale through your nose for a slow count of four, then hold your breath for a count of seven, and exhale through your nose for a count of eight. When you exhale, you will immediately feel yourself relax and let go of whatever is haunting you. When I do this, I feel my muscles loosen up and the knots in my stomach begin to unwind.

Your mind might start to be swept away by circular thought patterns of worry, but the counting forces you to focus. Say to yourself, "Inhale for four . . . three . . . two . . . one. Hold for seven . . . six . . . five . . . four . . . three . . . two . . . one. Exhale for eight . . . seven . . . six . . .

4-7-8 Breathing

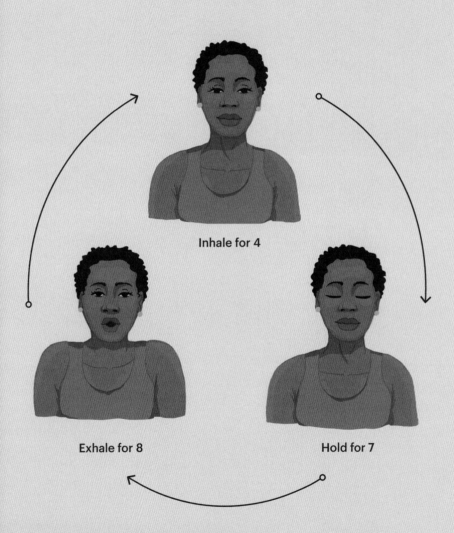

Inhale for 4

Hold for 7

Exhale for 8

five . . . four . . . three . . . two . . . one." If you lose count, calmly begin again. Rather than scolding yourself, be gentle and understanding because you know that you have a lot on your mind. It's okay if you get distracted. Just begin again.

This phrase *begin again* has stuck with me ever since my first ten-day silent-meditation retreat. It was an intense eleven hours of meditating every day for ten days without talking, and I remember the beginning of each session, when I heard the voice of the teacher say, "Begin again." It didn't matter that yesterday was a really hard day and my back hurt from sitting cross-legged on the floor for that long. It didn't matter that in the morning session my mind was wandering all over the place and I felt like I was doing it all wrong. Every time I sat down, I had the opportunity to begin again.

When you first start trying these breathing techniques, you might find it hard to focus, especially when you are using them in the most dire circumstances. Have patience with yourself, and remember to "begin again." Over time your ability to focus on the breath will strengthen like a muscle. The more you do it, the easier it will be, and the benefits will be amazing. In the morning, you will wake up feeling rested and ready for the day!

You can't control when anxiety will creep up on you or when that part of your brain just won't let you go to sleep. However, when it happens, you have the power to release yourself from its grip.

The Extra Workload

Sometimes being the only Black person at work means taking on responsibilities outside of your job description. You might be assigned administrative tasks like ordering lunch or event planning, when you were actually hired to be a data analyst, lawyer, or investor. This might make you feel like your company doesn't value your intelligence and all the amazing skills that you bring to the organization. You might also be pulled into diversity, equity, and inclusion initiatives, resulting in a significant amount of extra work. If you are passionate about these initiatives, you might enjoy it. However, it can feel unjust, because your work performance will be compared with that of your white colleagues who aren't required to spend time on these additional projects. In addition to the time required, the extra work often puts us in triggering situations that can be emotionally taxing as well. We might feel uncomfortable doing what's asked of us. Although the organization might have gotten what it wanted, we are left to heal from anger, resentment, sadness, and the huge range of emotions that come with its seemingly innocuous requests.

Though my actual roles have ranged from marketing to business development to product management, I have spent hours helping talent-acquisition teams develop strategies to attract and hire diverse employees. I have also been asked to attend significantly more recruiting events than my white colleagues. Companies like to showcase their diversity, but when you alone are their "diversity," that means that you have to go to all the events. I remember that at one company in particular I was supposed to enthusiastically tell everyone why it was so great to work there. Although there were many positive aspects to the job, I had to lie (through omission) about what it was like to be a Black person working there. This, too, was exhausting and just felt wrong. I was mad that none of my white colleagues had to spend as much time on recruiting as I did, and yet our workloads were equally rigorous. I had to stay up later to finish my work because of these events, and I felt like it just wasn't fair.

Have you ever felt like you were being "voluntold" to participate in diversity initiatives at work? Whenever you're asked to help, you might have mixed feelings. On the one hand, you want to do your part to drive change. You might feel like it's your duty as a Black person to do everything you can to pave the way for those who come after you. On the other hand, you might consider the near-term impact on your mental and physical health. There are only a certain number of hours in the day, and to do these extra tasks and your regular job means that something is going to suffer. For me, sleep is the first thing to go.

I desperately want to get it all done, and I will just choose to sleep less. However, studies show that insufficient sleep has been linked to weakened immunity, high blood pressure, memory issues, mood changes, and even a higher risk of getting into car accidents.

Rather than saying yes immediately, a mindful approach to these extra tasks would be to pause and ask yourself, "What will the impact be on my well-being, and is it worth it?" Sometimes the answer might be yes, sometimes it might be no, but at least you will be making the decision with intention.

I was often asked to facilitate discussions on race and speak publicly about my own personal racial traumas with my colleagues, even though I was not trained in doing so. There are people who do this for a living, and yet because I was Black it was assumed that I had this skill. Leading these discussions requires the ability to not internalize what is said. Similar to therapists' and social workers' jobs, it requires the ability to not bring triggering comments home with you in order to protect your own mental health.

I usually accepted these assignments without thinking about it. I wanted to be a team player and show my colleagues that I was willing to do whatever I could to make the organization a better place. On one particular occasion, this backfired and left me in tears, lying on the concrete in an alley behind my house, unable to move because I was so upset. I had worked up enough courage to publicly share my experiences of overt racism with my colleagues and how they had affected me. After I had spoken, there was time allocated for a facilitated discussion, and one of my colleagues said, "I'm from the alt-right, and I believe that the issue here is Black people's racism against white people and the violence that Black people have inflicted on the white race." I knew that these opinions existed in the world, but I was naive in believing that these opinions couldn't possibly have existed among the people that I worked with. I cried and cried. I was frozen in shock and disillusionment. I couldn't focus on anything. How could the people I worked with believe this? How could they have put me in the position to deal with this in the first place?

After three long days of feeling sorry for myself and feeling sad about the world, something clicked inside me. I realized that I didn't have to have to say yes. I realized that I had a secret power that I could use anytime that I needed to: the power to say no. An amazing author and teacher, adrienne maree brown, taught me that "No" is a complete sentence. Full stop. It's not "No, because . . ." or "No, but. . . ." It's okay to just say "No." Period. I realized that they would take what I let them take. But, we, Black people, have agency. We can say no, and they will just have to deal with it. I wasn't getting paid any extra money for this pain. Going through this didn't help drive my career forward. And if I said no, what's the worst that would happen? They could ask someone else. Or they could (gasp) pay a professional to do this extra work. A year later I was asked to speak at another company-wide event about the same topic, and can you guess what I said?

Do you automatically say yes to things that might make you uncomfortable? In what past situations could you have said no for your own well-being and self-care? Mindfulness means paying attention in the present moment to how you are feeling. The most important thing to do is to pause and pay attention. If your gut says no, then listen to it. Because of my upbringing, I have always had problems saying no. If you have similar challenges, I invite you to practice in the mirror.

When you first try doing mirror work, you might find it hard to take yourself seriously. However, be gentle with yourself in the process. Go to a mirror, take a deep breath, look into your own eyes, and say this out loud: "No."

Now imagine a white colleague asking you to do something you really don't want to do, and say it again, out loud: "No."

My first experience with this was challenging. Saying no was so foreign to me, I had a hard time even forming the word with my mouth. My first attempt was extremely tentative. I said it like it was a question. "Nooooo?" I said slowly. My voice increased in pitch as the word continued. I didn't even believe myself.

If you have this experience, take another deep breath and say to yourself, "I can do this. It doesn't matter who they are, they don't own me."

Now try it again. You might say it more matter-of-factly but still softly. Can your "No" be persuaded to say "Yes"?

If so, close your eyes and take one more deep breath. Call on your inner strength. Call on your ability to take care of yourself. Call on the willpower that you know you have inside you. Now open your eyes, blink, look directly into your eyes in the mirror, and say in a loud and unapologetic voice, "*No!*"

I went through this process, and, when I was finally able to say it with full confidence, that was it. From then on, I would practice my "No" in the mirror before going into a meeting and saying it. I still couched it in the pleasantries required for corporate social interactions; however, the message was clear and I would not let myself be persuaded.

The first time I used my secret power of "No," I had the president of an organization, an older white man, apologizing to me, and feeling guilty for asking in the first place. That's when I knew I was on to something. If you've never tried it, I invite you to do so in a situation that doesn't have any serious consequences and just see how it feels. It can be extremely liberating, especially when it's something you really didn't want to do but felt some irrational form of obligation to say yes to.

Sometimes you might pause to think about it and decide that you do want to say yes to certain requests that come your way. Knowing that these tasks will take a lot out of you, you decide to do them because they're worth it. For instance, I agreed to join a task force focused on improving opportunities for people of color at my company because I really wanted to drive change. I remember one week when I felt like I was underwater with my day job's workload, and I was responsible for putting together a presentation for senior management on diversity initiatives. I was exhausted, because, as I mentioned, sleep is what usually goes out the window for me in these circumstances. I still had so much to do, but I felt like I had expended all the energy that I had. Mary-Frances Winters coined the term *Black fatigue*, and, when I first

Bellows Breath

Inhale

Exhale

Exhale

Inhale

heard it, I thought to myself, *Wow! Finally a name for what I've been experiencing! We are tired!*

When you're exhausted, your go-to strategy might be to double or even triple your caffeine intake. Double-shot espressos might lead to jolts of energy followed by huge crashes in the middle of the day, which never feel good. However, I want to introduce you to a breathing technique that was extremely effective at boosting my energy levels during that week when I felt like I didn't have anything left. It's called the Bellows Breath*. I invite you to give it a try.

Be sure to do this on an empty stomach. Find yourself a comfortable position, either seated or standing, with your back straight. Make loose fists and hold them at your shoulders, with your elbows resting against your ribs. With a forceful and audible inhalation through your nose, quickly straighten your arms and shoot your hands into the air, opening your fists as if you were going to give high fives to friends. Then, with a forceful and audible exhalation through your nose, pull your elbows back down next to your ribs, with loose fists next to your shoulders once more.

Inhale and straighten your arms, opening your hands above your head into a high-five position once more. Make sure that your breath is forceful enough for you to hear it. Exhale through your nose as you bring your hands down and back into loose fists next to your shoulders, elbows next to your ribs. Each round of inhaling and exhaling should be quite fast, taking about one second per breath cycle. Every breath should pass in and out through the nose, and always forcefully enough to be audible.

Take ten breaths like this, and pause to see how you feel. Do it again, this time for twenty breaths. Pause once again to observe your body and observe your mind. Do one last round, again for twenty breaths. Close your eyes to check in once again. How are you feeling?

This practice can take some time and repetition to get used to. Some people feel a bit dizzy or light-headed when they first try it. If this happens to you, be sure to take longer breaks between rounds, and know that this feeling fades the more you do it.

* Bellows Breath is inspired by the traditional *Bhastrika pranayama*.

When I do the Bellows Breath, I can feel endorphins kicking in that typically come from doing cardio at the gym. The sluggishness I felt when I started already begins to disappear. Sometimes I feel so energized that I could run a marathon. After the third round, I always feel ready for the day and anything that might come my way.

If you're ever exhausted from all that gets placed on your shoulders, whether it's in the morning or a later, low-energy point in your day, I invite you to try the Bellows Breath. It's healthier than coffee and has a much longer-lasting effect.

The Opportunity

Although being the only Black person comes with its challenges, it can be helpful to reframe the situation as an opportunity. Rather than thinking about how you *have* to deal with all that comes with it (the extra work, the extra responsibility, the extra weight), I invite you to think about all that you *get* to do as "the only." When you are the only Black person, what does this *allow* you to do? What can you do in this situation that you might not otherwise?

A couple years ago I found myself at some hot springs in Oregon. I was surrounded by an array of deep green ferns, listening to the sound of a waterfall flowing into a small pool created by a magical rock formation. My entire body was submerged in the natural warmth of healing mineral waters, and I was in absolute bliss. Suddenly I opened my eyes and looked around to realize that I was the only Black person in this pool. And then I realized that I hadn't seen any Black people since I arrived. At first my natural defense mechanisms kicked in like clockwork. Survival instincts are real. My thoughts started to spiral. *What am I doing here? Why do I always end up in these situations? Are these people secret racists? Are they staring at me? Oregon's history with Black people is pretty bleak. Am I safe? Is something going to happen to me in the middle of the night?*

If you ever get caught in these endless thought patterns, mindfulness can be extremely powerful. The first step is to notice that it's happening. When you notice, then you can do something about it. Say to yourself, "I am experiencing a spiral of negativity" or "I am experiencing an emotionally triggering moment." Whatever you are experiencing, naming it and describing it as an experience allows you to separate yourself from the thoughts themselves. You are not these thoughts, and you have the agency to influence where they go. Start with some deep breaths as a first step toward taking control of the experience. Then think about how you can reframe this situation as an opportunity.

Yes, I was the only Black person at these hot springs, but what did this enable me to do? If I had not gone because I didn't want to be the only Black person there, I would not have been able to experience the magic of this place. The birds sang songs of peace. The sunset over the tree line opened my heart in ways I can't describe. The smell of the moist earth and the pine trees gave me a profound sense of grounding. *This* was why I was here, and it was absolutely worth it.

In corporate settings, being "the only" allows you to be a voice that wouldn't ordinarily be heard. When you're asked the question "What do Black people think?" you might be triggered and find yourself engaging in an angry internal dialogue. *I am not all Black people. We are not a monolith. Why would you think that I would know what all Black people think?* However, you can be the voice that explains the flaw in the question to begin with. Although it's exhausting to constantly educate people on their ignorance, you get to move them one step forward in their thinking.

A few years ago I was in a managers' meeting discussing team performance and the low representation of African Americans and Latinos in leadership roles. A white colleague said, "They just don't want to get promoted. We want to promote them, but they just aren't motivated to move up." If I were not in the room, I'm sure that would have been the end of the conversation. They would have felt good that they had talked about it and "tried," but nothing would have been done. Instead, as the only Black person present, I was able to share the challenges that come with being a person of color in the workplace. I talked about imposter syndrome, the lack of mentors that look like us, and the talent they were missing out on by not fostering an environment where we could succeed. This led to some proactive initiatives to make changes in the organization.

As the only Black person in a leadership role, you get to proactively drive change regarding the hiring and promoting of people of color. You get to be a formal and informal mentor to Black people who are more junior in the organization. This is the opportunity. This is what you *get* to do.

The next time you find that you are "the only," ask yourself this question:

"What is the opportunity here?"

Key Points to Remember

- When you are "the only," count on your community outside this situation for comfort and validation. A simple phone call or text message from someone who understands can be life-changing. Who can you call for support?

- The ability to focus on the breath is like a muscle; it's hard at first, but over time, with more practice and use, you can and will build that strength.

- Begin again. If you get distracted when you're trying to breathe or create some space for calm in your life, remember to be kind to yourself and know that you can always begin again.

- Before saying yes to everything asked of you, especially in the workplace, be sure to pause and ask yourself if this is really something you want to do. Listen to your gut.

Mindfulness Practice Toolkit

Mindfulness Practice 17: 4-7-8 Breathing

When you are experiencing anxiety or having trouble falling asleep because of the intense pressure to be flawless in your performance:

1 Exhale and empty your lungs.

2 Inhale through your nose for four seconds, counting "four . . . three . . . two . . . one" in your mind.

3 Hold the breath for seven seconds, counting "seven . . . six . . . five . . . four . . . three . . . two . . . one."

4 Exhale through your nose for eight seconds, counting "eight . . . seven . . . six . . . five . . . four . . . three . . . two . . . one."

5 Repeat at least five times; the longer you practice, the greater the calm you will experience.

Mindfulness Practice 18: The Power of No

When you are being asked to do things that make you uncomfortable or that are more than you have the bandwidth for:

1 Pause and ask yourself, "Do I want to do this? Do I have the space to do this? What will the impact be on me and on others if I do this?" Listen to your gut.

2 If the answer is no, and you find it challenging to verbalize it, consider practicing in the mirror. Look directly into your own eyes, and say "No" firmly. If this doesn't come easily to you, take a deep breath, and try again. Each time, try to say it louder and with a more definitive tone.

3 Now imagine the person asking you to do this thing that you don't want to do, and then practice saying "No" in your response.

4 Practice saying "No" in a real-life situation that doesn't have any major consequences and see how it feels.

Mindfulness Practice 19: Bellows Breath[*]

When you are feeling exhausted, whether it's in the morning or during a slump in the middle of the day:

1 Make loose fists with your hands, and hold them at your shoulders, with your elbows resting against your ribs.

2 With a forceful and audible inhalation through your nose, quickly straighten your arms and shoot your hands up into the air, opening your fists as if to give high fives to friends.

3 With a forceful and audible exhalation through your nose, pull your elbows back down next to your ribs and make loose fists next to your shoulders once more.

4 Repeat steps 2 and 3 with rapid and audible inhalations and exhalations, with each round of inhaling and exhaling lasting about

[*] Do not practice Bellows Breath if you are pregnant or have a medical history of hypertension, epilepsy, seizures, or panic attacks. Avoid practicing on a full stomach.

one second. Be sure to breathe in and out through your nose, so that you can hear each breath loudly.

5 Do one round of this for ten breaths.

6 Pause for fifteen to thirty seconds and see how you feel.

7 Do a second round for twenty breaths.

8 Pause for fifteen to thirty seconds and see how you feel.

9 Do a third round for twenty breaths.

10 Pause for fifteen to thirty seconds and see how you feel.

Mindfulness Practice 20: "I Get to . . ."

When you find yourself frustrated or uncomfortable because you are "the only":

1 Close your eyes and take a deep breath.

2 Consider how you might be able to reframe this experience as an opportunity.

3 In your journal, write at the top of a new page, "I get to . . ."

4 Make a list of all of the things you get to do because you are in this situation that you wouldn't have been able to do otherwise.

CHAPTER EIGHT

R-E-S-P-E-C-T
at Work

**I'm not concerned with your liking or disliking me.
All I ask is that you respect me as a human being.**

—Jackie Robinson,
first African American Major League Baseball player

*When we, Black people, achieve success in the workplace, being
treated with respect by our colleagues is not a given.* Microaggressions
might feel like an everyday occurrence. People might question our
competence. Our compensation might not be aligned with our job title
and experience. We might not be taken seriously by our teams, and
sometimes we might feel invisible. If we do work up the courage to
address our concerns with Human Resources (HR), they often dismiss
us as overly sensitive.

I was giving a private breathwork session to a Black woman who
had risen through the ranks at a prestigious investment firm. When

I asked her what challenges she wanted to address with breathwork, she said that her work environment was so toxic that she was debating whether to stick it out or leave, even though she loved the work itself.

As tears rolled down her cheeks, she told me about an incident in which she had asked her younger, white, male direct reports to update the numbers on some important documents that would be released publicly. They felt like she was asking too much (when this was a pretty standard ask in the industry), and they proceeded to throw pens and balled-up pieces of paper at her during the meeting. The next day she went to HR to help address the matter, but the guilty parties were out of the office. The entire team (all white males), including the managing directors and partners, those both above and below her in seniority, were at a golf outing. Not only was she not invited, they hadn't even bothered to tell her they would be out of the office. She was working hard, as Black women typically are, and the entire team was out playing golf. It was as if she didn't exist.

When white people report to us, they sometimes treat us differently than they do other managers because they might not be accustomed to this power dynamic. I was leading a team during a very stressful time for our company, and it was not unusual for the CEO to yell at the leadership team and bang his fists on the table during meetings. My group was leading an initiative that was expected to provide a new revenue stream to counter the slowed growth the company was experiencing. I'm always very aware of being perceived as the "angry Black woman," so I'm never one to yell or bang my fists when leading a team. However, having grown up on the East Coast, I am very direct with my feedback. If there are opportunities for improvement, I will tell you in real time what those are. The pressure was on for all of us, and I had high expectations for my team. Time was not on our side, and every week I had to report back what we had achieved. Although it's difficult to honestly assess oneself, I can say with confidence that my management style wasn't even on the same scale of "aggressive" as that of others in the company's leadership.

So, when I heard that a few people who reported to me had joined forces to complain to HR, I was taken aback. The feedback was that I was extremely aggressive, that I was too demanding, and that they wanted me to praise them more. Although we all have areas in which we can improve, I couldn't help but wonder whether they would have given this feedback if I were a white man.

I knew the power of white voices, and I was terrified of losing my job. I felt humiliated because even though I was the boss, they held the power. Another Black woman at our company had been fired for being too vocal, and I felt like I was walking on eggshells. I became overly conscious of my tone and very aware of every word that came out of my mouth. I tried to channel a white preschool teacher's voice—"Great job, Bobby! You're amazing!"—even when this was not the case. I was so anxious that I couldn't sleep. I would wake up at two a.m. from a nightmare in which I was surrounded by their faces, and they were holding torches and pitchforks.

This felt like an example of *career lynching*, a term coined by a friend of mine at a leading tech company. She had received a big promotion, and a white woman who reported to her was mad that she did not also get one, so she made up stories for HR to try to get my friend fired. Ida B. Wells described lynching as "an excuse to get rid of Negroes who were acquiring wealth and property and thus keep the race terrorized and 'keep the n***** down.'" Have you ever felt this way at work?

After receiving this feedback, I decided to face it head-on. I held a meeting with my team to create an open forum for discussion of their issues. Although this approach might sound like a very calm way to handle it, I assure you that this was not the case. My heart was racing during the hours and minutes leading up to this meeting. I felt like I was walking directly into a fire to be burned at the stake. I cried so many tears because I felt helpless in this reverse power dynamic. I was an emotional wreck, and I didn't know if I was going to be able to keep it together as I stood in front of them.

This is when I used my breathwork training to greatest effect.

The night before the meeting, the morning of the meeting, and even minutes before it, I did a powerful breathing technique for grounding and creating a sense of balance. It's called Alternate-Nostril Breathing*. Studies have shown that it reduces stress levels and improves heart rate, respiratory rate, and blood pressure. My stress levels were through the roof and my heart started racing when I imagined myself in this meeting. Every time I felt this, I would find a quiet place alone and start my breathing exercise.

If you can relate to this level of stress, give this a try. Close your right nostril completely with your right thumb. Inhale deeply through your left nostril. Close your left nostril with your right ring finger. Remove your right thumb from your right nostril, and exhale through your right nostril. Inhale deeply through your right nostril, close your right nostril with your thumb, release your left nostril, and slowly and deeply exhale through your left nostril. Inhale through your left nostril once again, and use your ring finger to close your left nostril. Remove your thumb from your right nostril, and exhale through your right nostril once again. Continue this pattern of inhaling on one side, closing that nostril, and exhaling through the opposite side, for at least five rounds. I consider one round as having inhaled and exhaled from each side. If you have more time, do this for five to ten minutes. Although the shorter sessions have an immediate effect on my nerves, when I sit for longer I am able to find a deeper sense of calm. My heart rate slows and my body relaxes, especially my shoulders, where I typically hold a lot of tension.

These few minutes of Alternate-Nostril Breathing reminded me that, although I couldn't control a lot of things in my environment, my breath was something that I did have control over. I walked into the room breathing deeply. I stood in front of them and calmly said, "I understand that some of you expressed concern about my management style, and I want to make sure that this is a fulfilling and rewarding environment for each and every one of you. I would like to hear your concerns, and it would be helpful for me to hear specific examples in order to make sure they are addressed."

* Alternate-Nostril Breathing Is inspired by the traditional *Nadi Shodhana pranayama*.

Alternate-Nostril Breathing

Close your right nostril

Exhale through your left nostril

Inhale through your left

Close your left nostril

Open your right nostril, and exhale through your right

Inhale through your right nostril

Repeat from the top, at least 5 more times

In my mind, I was thinking, *Phew! I said it!* Rather than acting defensive and slipping into fight-or-flight-or-freeze mode, breathing beforehand had allowed me to channel the kindest, most empathetic voice I could, so that they could feel like they were heard. Although I was open to feedback, and always aware that there are areas in which I could improve, this felt like a group of white people coming for me, so I had to be extremely intentional about staying calm. Overall, the meeting went well; however, the boss that they wanted me to be, the white preschool teacher, ultimately required too much of my energy.

People often use the term *microaggressions* to describe situations like this. *Microaggression* is defined by *Merriam-Webster's Dictionary* as

> a comment or action that *subtly* and often *unconsciously* or *unintentionally* expresses a prejudiced attitude toward a member of a marginalized group.

I highlight the words *subtly*, *unconsciously*, and *unintentionally*, because this is what defines these events as "micro." When my team went to HR to complain about me and I felt like my livelihood was threatened, it didn't feel very "micro" to me! *Macroaggressions* typically refer to large-scale or overt aggression toward those of a different race, culture, or gender, and when you take what happened to me, what happened to my friend, and what's happening probably at this moment to many Black people at work, *macro* feels much more appropriate.

That said, our white colleagues might not share the same perspective because they are rarely on the receiving end. I work with Black employee resource groups at Fortune 500 companies to help their communities heal from microaggressions in the workplace. One of my clients shared that their company had decided that the term *microaggressions* was too aggressive, so they officially declared that instead they would call them "Ouch, it hurts." Their 100,000 employees were instructed to describe these debilitating events that cause us high blood pressure, anxiety, depression, and so much more, with a phrase used by a toddler when they scrape their knee.

Although we might not be able to make the white people in power understand the gravity of the impact they have on our mental, emotional, and physical health, we can exercise agency by healing ourselves when we are attacked at work, whether they call them microaggressions or an "Ouch, it hurts." Microaggressions and macroaggressions come in many forms, and I will share a few examples that you may have experienced in the workplace in some capacity.

Having Your Competence Questioned

According to Lean In's study, *The State of Black Women in Corporate America*, 40 percent of Black women feel that they need to provide more evidence of their competence, compared to 14 percent of white men. Though this is an alarming statistic, it was comforting to know that I wasn't alone. I learned this lesson very early in my career. I was responsible for a lot of data analysis, and I noticed that when my white colleagues made comments, they were immediately praised. When I made comments, I was asked significantly more questions about my methodology, and I was always asked for the supporting data. The first time it happened, I didn't have it at my fingertips, even though I had done thorough research and analysis. Every time after that, knowing the questions would come for me and no one else in the room, I made sure to be overprepared and I always had the backup for everything I said.

Although I've come to expect this extra grilling in meetings, and I'm now always prepared, it makes me feel like I'm not enough. It makes me feel like my colleagues don't trust me or my work. As soon as the question is asked, I feel myself cringe. If you find yourself having this experience, remember to breathe to keep yourself calm and grounded. The extra-long exhalation described in chapter 5 is useful in these moments. Every time someone questions my competence, I take an extra-long exhalation. It's something so subtle that they won't notice even though they are sitting right across from me, and it allows me to release whatever emotion was triggered in the moment so that I can immediately bring back my "A game" and calmly respond.

Not Getting Promoted

Being passed over for a promotion is always frustrating, but when you're Black it can often feel like an intentional oversight—especially when you've already been taking on additional responsibility and excelling in your current position. According to the U.S. Equal Employment Opportunity Commission, Black professionals account for only 3 percent of executive or senior leadership roles. Our colleagues might put this in the microaggression category because it is "unconscious" or "unintentional," but the impact is very real. Not only does it affect our confidence, it also affects our earning potential, our overall career trajectory, and, on a larger scale, the socioeconomic trajectory of our entire community.

Several years ago, my boss moved on to another role, and I took over all her responsibilities for leading the team and selling to corporate clients. I diligently did her job for six months, but during this time I found that, although potential clients were expressing interest, they wanted to meet only with someone with a more senior title. I worked up enough courage to ask my boss for a promotion. I provided him with concrete evidence about why I deserved it, the accomplishments I'd led the team to achieve, and the fact that I was essentially already doing the job. I also told him that he was losing a significant amount of revenue because my job title was preventing him from winning major deals.

He agreed that I was doing a great job, that I deserved a promotion, and that he didn't want to lose any additional business because of this. However, he shared that, due to a leveling exercise that HR was conducting, he couldn't offer me a formal promotion. Instead he instructed me to change my title on LinkedIn and have new business cards printed with the new title. That way, we would be able to get these big deals and no revenue would be lost. But this solution meant that I would not receive the additional compensation that aligned with my responsibilities and workload.

I sat there in this meeting, stunned at the response. Although I felt validated for my contributions and abilities, I also felt shafted. I had watched young white men be promoted at exponential speeds. I saw exceptions being made for them on a regular basis, and often it wasn't clear to me that the pace of their promotions aligned with their contributions. I was clearly being treated differently than my white colleagues, and I felt like there was nothing I could do about it. So, I swallowed my pride and took it. I gave myself a fake promotion on LinkedIn and I had new business cards printed, as instructed. Everyone, including my colleagues, my direct reports, and my clients, believed that I had this higher title. However, behind the scenes, only the CEO, HR, and I knew the truth. Although they would call it a temporary fix (which lasted an entire year), I had one word for it:

Racism.

My parents taught me at a young age that life wasn't fair. They taught me that you had to play the hand that you were dealt. Survival is important, especially for people of color in America. However, what they didn't teach me was self-care. The night after my boss told me he would so generously offer me a fake promotion, I could feel myself getting more and more upset about being mistreated. I was so mad that I wanted to scream! I knew I needed to release this, that holding in these feelings was only going to make it and me worse. I had once been taught a technique that I call Squeeze and Release, and that night before I went to bed I took some time to eject this anger from my body.

The next time you experience a similar feeling, close your eyes and inhale deeply. Then hold your breath and squeeze every muscle in your body. Curl your fingers into the tightest fists you can make. Squeeze your butt muscles. Scrunch up your face. Curl your toes. Squeeze your biceps. Squeeze your calf muscles. Contract every single muscle in your body, and hold your breath and your body in that position for five seconds. Then let it all go. Exhale with a long and vocal "Haaaaaaa." Let your muscles relax and hang loose. When you are ready, do it again. Squeeze every muscle, scrunch up your face, make tight fists, and repeat the exercise, this time for ten seconds, because this level of anger might need the turbo treatment. As you count, squeeze harder the closer you get to "ten." Squeeze with all your rage. Squeeze with every part of your being that wants to be free from this prison of constantly being belittled and undervalued. When you get to "ten," let it all go with an even longer "Haaaaaaaaaaaaaaaaa," and let your exhalation linger for as long as you can.

Sometimes you might feel a little light-headed if you squeeze extra-hard, but know that this is moving some really big energy around in your body. Be gentle with yourself. Consider lying down to rest afterward or listening to some calming music for five to ten minutes to facilitate a longer-term release of that which no longer serves you.

When I did this, I felt my body melt into my chair. I felt my feet sink into the earth. I felt my shoulders release a deep pain, an ancient pain that I didn't realize had been with me for a very long time. I sat there, so relaxed. The weight of that negative energy had been lifted and I could move more freely without it. It didn't change the situation, but it did help me to feel a *lot* better. I'm not sure I could have gone to work the next day with my head held high without having done it. And every time this pissed-off feeling would come up I would do it again. These practices are not one-time solutions; they are to be used whenever difficult emotions arise.

Feeling Ignored and Invisible

Sometimes being Black at work can make us feel invisible, like the people around us just aren't hearing us or seeing us. Here's a scenario that I've experienced so many times in my career that I've come to expect it.

Squeeze and Release

Take a deep breath in

At the top of the inhalation,
squeeze every muscle in
your body

Hold for 5 seconds ━━━━━━━━━━━━━━━

Exhale slowly and relax

I make a comment in a meeting. No one acknowledges my comment, and they move on as if nothing were said. Then a white man makes the exact same point, and he is applauded for his contribution. The first time this happened, I thought I was crazy. *Did that just happen? Did anyone else notice that he just stole my point? Did no one hear me?*

I teach mindfulness for Black employees across the country to heal from racism at work. At one of my workshops at a large global company, every single person in attendance had experienced this scenario. Because it is the norm to appear strong, it is rare for us to discuss these things when they happen. I conduct polls during my workshops so that people can see that we are not alone. If this has happened to you, I want you to know that this is not all in your head.

Psychologists have been studying this for several years, and they have assigned some very technical-sounding words to this phenomenon. The theory of *nonprototypicality* suggests that, because we do not fit into their box, they just don't see us. *Intersectional invisibility* is the idea that "possessing multiple subordinate-group identities can render people 'invisible' relative to those with a single [subordinate-]group identity because the former are perceived as non-prototypical members of their respective identity groups." In simpler terms, white people are the single-group identity; they are the "prototype." Black people fall outside of the prototype, and as a result we are invisible to them.

Amanda Sesko and Monica Biernat conducted two studies to "address whether Black women go 'unnoticed' and their voices 'unheard' by examining memory for Black women's faces and speech contributions." They found that white people were least likely to accurately recognize Black women's faces compared to the faces of other groups. In addition, they found that when Black women made statements in group discussions, they were the least likely to get any attribution. Meaning that if a Black woman says something in a meeting, what she said would be remembered, but white people wouldn't remember that it was *she* who said it. However, if a white person says something, there is a much higher likelihood that what they said will get the correct attribution. I have often felt invisible at work, and this study shows that I'm not crazy. I can't tell you the relief I felt when I found that it wasn't just me.

However, it doesn't make it hurt any less when I don't feel seen. On my last day on a job, the chief marketing officer of the company asked me for a final meeting, in which she said to me, "How does it feel to know that the only thing people are talking about is that a Black woman just quit?" I had dedicated nights and weekends to this company. I had made this company millions of dollars and sacrificed my personal life and my emotional well-being for the sake of its profits. Instead of seeing my contributions to the company's growth, instead of seeing me as an individual, she informed me that what everyone cared about was the PR headline—BLACK WOMAN QUITS.

I was so angry that she had the audacity to say this to me. I was even more upset that perhaps the statement was true. No matter how hard I worked, no matter what I achieved, I would just be "a Black woman" in their eyes. Malcolm X once asked, "What does a white man call a black man with a PhD?" The answer? "A n***** with a PhD." Although I didn't have a PhD, I had two degrees from Harvard, I had a proven track record of driving revenue and growth across multiple industries, and this parallel didn't seem too far off.

When you feel like they just don't see you, they don't respect you, and they don't value you, you may experience feelings of frustration, anger, and resentment that can be hard to shake. Nelson Mandela said, "Resentment is like drinking poison and then hoping it will kill your enemies." I have experienced so many health problems, from insomnia to precancerous cells in my body, as a result of not being seen. Releasing this anger has allowed me to truly heal. A breathwork technique called the Breath of Fire has helped me to do just that[*]. In addition to releasing anger, this technique releases toxins and chemicals from the cells in your body, boosts your immune system, delivers more oxygen to your brain (which improves your ability to focus), and so much more.

[*] Breath of Fire is inspired by the traditional *Kapalbhati pranayama*.

Whenever you get really angry, here's what you can do. Focus on the event and the feeling that you need to release. Place a hand on your belly and take one long, deep inhalation through your nose so that your belly fills up completely. Then use your abdominal muscles to quickly and forcefully pump air out with rapid and repeated exhalations through your nose. Your exhalations should be loud, powerful, and fast. Don't worry about inhaling in the middle of the exhalations, because your body will naturally take in oxygen. Instead, focus on using your stomach muscles to pump the air out with repeated exhalations. With your hand on your belly, you can feel your stomach working as it comes back toward your spine on each exhalation.

When you first try this technique, after one long inhalation do ten forceful and fast exhalations just to get a sense of what it feels like. Once you get the hang of it, increase the number of rapid exhalations, first to twenty, then to thirty, and all the way up to sixty if you can!

When the anger runs super-deep and it's affecting your entire being, you can do a modified and more physical version of the traditional Breath of Fire technique to really get it out of your system. Start with your hands in fists, and your arms raised straight to the sky. Take a long, deep inhalation through your nose. Begin a series of rapid exhalations, and with each exhalation bring your elbows down to your sides and squeeze your ribs with your elbows. When you start every exhalation, begin with your fists raised straight above your head, and then with a loud and forceful exhalation bring your elbows down to squeeze your ribs forcefully. Straighten your arms up toward the sky again, and with every exhalation bring your elbows down with a force and intention to match your desire to get rid of this feeling and to get this anger out of your body. Remember that these should be quick exhalations through your nose, and you should be able to hear the sound of your exhalation. Start with ten breaths, and gradually increase the number as you feel comfortable.

When you first try this, you might feel dizzy, tingly, or light-headed. Know that this is normal, and it will happen less and less the

Enhanced Breath of Fire

Loud, fast exhalations through the nose

more you practice. It is also important to take a few minutes to lie down afterward to rest. Drink a lot of water throughout the day because this technique is releasing a lot of toxins and incredibly powerful emotions.

While lying down after the exercise, I experienced a sense of peace that I had never quite experienced before. It was like all that I was holding had been released, and I could finally relax. If you need to release some anger, I invite you to give this a try.

When It Just Feels Like Too Much

Sometimes all the things that happen at work can feel like too much to handle. We can feel overwhelmed, discouraged, and even defeated. In these moments I utilize two very different approaches for picking myself back up. The first I like to refer to as "Black Love as Medicine." Sometimes immersing myself in a community of people that look like me can be just the medicine that I need to feel better, because they understand what I'm going through, because I don't need to put on an act around them. In the workplace this can come in the form of Black employee resource groups. It can also come in the form of Black mentors or friends, either at your company or externally. I have been leading mindfulness groups for Black and brown communities for the past few years, and being in these safe spaces with people with open hearts and an intention for mutual support can be incredibly powerful, even when they are online. Black Love as Medicine can also be used in the same way that we think about vitamins: Don't wait until it gets so bad that you feel overwhelmed. If you ensure that you have just a little bit on a regular basis, you have a higher likelihood of remaining healthy and happy, regardless of the challenges that arise.

The second approach I take is very physical, and it involves a practice our ancestors have been engaging in for generations: dance.

Dance has been used throughout the African diaspora as a tool to heal from trauma. Nicole Monteiro, psychologist and owner of the

Center for Healing and Development, explains that "dance is a physical behavior that embodies many curative properties that are released through movement, rhythms, self-expression, and communion, as well as the mechanisms of cathartic release. These properties allow individuals to shift emotional states, oftentimes creating an experience of wholeness."

When you've had a hard day, when you feel like you just can't handle it anymore, I invite you to do what I call a Conscious Dance Release. Choose some fast-paced music that you know will get you moving. For me, that's something with lots of percussion and energetic rhythms. Ideally the music doesn't have too many lyrics, which might tempt you to sing along. However, choose some music that you love that you know will get you dancing. I like to put on headphones so I can blast the music and be fully immersed in it without bothering anyone else in the building.

Close your eyes, and start by shaking every part of your body. Shake your hands, your arms, your legs. For me this eventually leads to a sort of jumping around, in which my body is shaking all on its own to its own natural rhythms merging with the music's. Shake for about a minute or two, and when you're ready, with your eyes still closed, begin to dance. There's no science to this. There is no proper form. This is your body doing what it needs to do, doing what it is drawn to do. No one is watching. It is a complete surrender to what the body needs to do, wants to do, right here, right now. Sometimes your body might go straight into really big motions. Allow yourself to take up space. Sometimes you might need to work up to it with smaller movements, but, regardless of where you start, eventually get big and take up space!

When I do this, it feels amazing. It's me letting me fully *be* me in this moment. I feel how it feels to move. I'm not trying to stay in control. I'm letting it be just as it is, dancing to the beats, letting my heart and my soul guide me.

After five to ten minutes of dancing (I'm usually exhausted after five, but that's just me), and with your eyes still closed, lie down for another five to ten minutes and let your entire body melt into the floor. Notice how you feel.

When I do this, my heart rate slows down. I feel at peace. I feel like I got something out, something that really needed to come out. When I get up, I immediately feel lighter. I feel like I have shed all the weight that was bringing me down. I come up from this resting position with the deep knowledge that I am bold, I am fierce, and I am my ancestors' wildest dreams.

Finally, when work life gets me down, Dr. Maya Angelou's words are always with me:

"Still I rise."

Key Points to Remember

- Although we might not be able to make white people understand the gravity of the impact that microaggressions have on our mental, emotional, and physical health, we can take responsibility for healing ourselves when we are attacked at work.

- It's important to be intentional about acknowledging and releasing anger about offensive situations. To repeat, Nelson Mandela said, "Resentment is like drinking poison and then hoping it will kill your enemies."

- Even before you get to the point of feeling overwhelmed, practice Black Love as Medicine, and immerse yourself in a community of people that look like you, such as Black employee resource groups, Black mentors and friends, or mindfulness groups for people of color.

- These practices are not one-time solutions; they should be used whenever any difficult situations and emotions arise.

Mindfulness Practice Toolkit

Mindfulness Practice 21: Alternate-Nostril Breathing[*]

Before walking into a meeting that you know will be stressful or triggering:

1 Close your right nostril with your right thumb.

2 Inhale through your left nostril.

3 Close your left nostril with your right ring finger.

4 Open your right nostril and exhale through it.

5 Inhale through your right nostril.

6 Close your right nostril with your right thumb.

7 Open your left nostril and exhale through it.

8 Return to step 2, and repeat the cycle of steps 2 through 7 at least five times, or for five to ten minutes if you have time.

(Note that if you are left-handed, you can use your left thumb and left ring finger to open and close your nostrils.)

[*] Alternate-Nostril Breathing should not be practiced while suffering from a cold, the flu, or a fever.

Mindfulness Practice 22: Squeeze and Release

When you are annoyed and frustrated because you feel like you're not being seen:

1 Focus your attention on the situation that is causing you to feel this way.

2 Inhale fully through your nose.

3 Hold your breath and squeeze all the muscles in your body—make fists and clench your toes, squeeze the muscles in your face, squeeze your thighs, your calf muscles—everything.

4 Hold for a count of five seconds.

5 Exhale with a long vocal "Haaaaaaaa" and relax.

6 Repeat three times.

Mindfulness Practice 23: Breath of Fire[*]

When you are feeling really angry about something that was said or done and you need to release it:

1 Focus on what you need to release.

2 Place a hand on your belly and inhale deeply through your nose.

3 Use your abdominal muscles to quickly, forcefully pump air out, with rapid and repeated exhalations through your nose.

4 Exhalations should be loud, powerful, and fast. Don't worry about inhaling in the middle of the exhalations because your body will naturally take in oxygen. Instead, focus on using your stomach muscles to pump the air out with each exhalation.

5 Continue without pausing for ten rapid exhalations.

6 Repeat steps 2 through 7 for three rounds, resting for at least thirty seconds between them.

7 As you get more experience with the technique, gradually increase to sixty rapid exhalations per round.

8 After completing the exercise, lie down for five to ten minutes and breathe naturally.

[*] Breath of Fire should not be practiced while pregnant, during menstruation, or if you suffer from vertigo, high blood pressure, heart disease, or seizures.

Mindfulness Practice 23B: Enhanced Breath of Fire

When the anger is extremely intense and all-consuming:

1 Focus on what you need to release.

2 Curl the fingers of both hands into fists.

3 Straighten your arms and raise your fists to the sky.

4 Inhale deeply through your nose.

5 Repeat a similar series of rapid exhalations as in Breath of Fire; however, with each exhalation bring your elbows down to your sides and squeeze your ribs with your elbows.

6 When you start every exhalation, have your arms and fists raised to the sky and then bring your elbows down to squeeze your ribs forcefully with the loud and forceful exhalation.

7 Bring your elbows down and squeeze your ribs with a force and intention that matches your desire to get this anger out of your body.

8 Do not worry about the inhalation, because your body will naturally inhale.

9 Exhalations should be loud, powerful, and fast.

10 Continue without pausing for ten rapid exhalations.

11 Repeat for three rounds, resting for at least thirty seconds between them.

12 As you get more experience with the technique, gradually increase to sixty rapid exhalations per round.

13 After completing the exercise, lie down for five to ten minutes and breathe naturally.

Mindfulness Practice 24: Conscious Dance Release
When you've had a hard day, and when you feel like you just can't handle any more:

1 Set a timer for at least five minutes.

2 Choose some fast-paced music that you love, and that you know will get you dancing. (Ideally it's music without too many lyrics that might tempt you to sing along.)

3 Consider wearing headphones so you can blast the music and be fully immersed without bothering your neighbors or housemates.

4 Close your eyes.

5 Start shaking every part of your body: your hands, your arms, your legs.

6 Allow your body to start moving and jumping to its own natural rhythms, merging with the music.

7 Shake for about a minute or two, and when you're ready, with your eyes still closed, begin to dance.

8 Surrender to what your body wants to do, right here, right now. Take up space.

9 When the timer goes off, turn off the music.

10 With your eyes closed, lie down for another five to ten minutes and let your entire body melt into the floor.

11 When you are ready, open your eyes, and see how you feel.

CHAPTER NINE

Countering Imposter Syndrome with Courage

Each time I write a book, every time I face that yellow pad, the challenge is so great. I have written eleven books, but each time I think, "Uh oh, they're going to find out now. I've run a game on everybody and they're going to find me out."

—Maya Angelou

The first time I experienced imposter syndrome, I was eight years old. It was my first day at an expensive private school in the suburbs of Washington, D.C., and I had received a scholarship based on my test scores and my family's financial circumstances. I lived far away in a predominantly Black, low-income neighborhood in D.C., with a slow, traffic-filled commute to get there. As my parents drove me down the long tree-lined driveway of what looked more like a castle than a school,

I noticed how nice and shiny the other cars were in the drop-off line. There were BMWs and Mercedeses, and some of the kids even had private drivers in uniform. Before I set foot in the building, I felt like I wasn't supposed to be there. When I entered my classroom, I looked around and realized that I was the only Black person in it. By the end of the first day, I knew that all these kids had private tutors and that they were way more prepared than I was for the academic rigor. They were already preparing for college, and we were only in elementary school! I felt like I wasn't smart enough or rich enough to be there. When were they going to find out that they had made a mistake and that I really didn't belong? I didn't know then, but I know now, that what I was experiencing was actually imposter syndrome.

American psychologists Pauline R. Clance and Suzanne A. Imes coined the term in 1978 as the "internal experience of intellectual phoniness in people who believe that they are not intelligent, capable or creative despite evidence of high achievement." Although they "are highly motivated to achieve," they also "live in fear of being 'found out' or exposed as frauds." Note that this is "internal." This is all happening in our minds, and what we are thinking has nothing to do with what others are thinking about us! When I first read this definition, I couldn't help but focus on the mention of "evidence." There are hard facts that directly contradict this feeling of self-doubt, yet we experience it anyway.

How can you tell whether you have experienced imposter syndrome? Although there are many symptoms, I will share the eight that really resonate with me. As I go through them, I invite you to take note of which of these you have experienced.

8 Symptoms of Imposter Syndrome

1 **"I'm a fake and I'm going to be found out."**
   This is how I felt on the first day of school when I was eight years old,
   but I also felt this way on my first day at a new job that I didn't feel
   like I was qualified for, and in so many other circumstances in my
   life! Have you ever felt this way?

2 **Hard to accept praise.**
   When I receive positive feedback, I usually discount it with an
   internal commentary like *They are just being nice or I just got lucky.*
   However, when I receive criticism, I repeat it over and over again in
   my mind, focusing on the negative like it's the only thing that matters, as if it defines me. How well do you accept praise?

3 **Inflexible goal setting.**
   Do you hold yourself to such incredibly high standards that the
   goalpost is unreachable, regardless of the circumstances? I often tell
   myself I'm not good enough and that I'm not worthy because I didn't
   meet a goal that no one could have possibly met!

4 **Perfectionism.**
   Related to inflexible goal setting, this is when we feel the need
   to work on something until it's absolutely perfect. We don't feel
   satisfied until we know "everything" about the subject because we
   need to prove that we really do belong. As a Black person, I feel like
   I have to work twice as hard and be twice as qualified as a white
   person, so the pressure is on! Can you relate?

5 **Intense fear of failure.**
   Are you scared to fail? Do you ever feel like failure is just not an
   option? Often I feel like there is so much pressure to succeed that
   if I don't perform at the highest level, my career and my life will be

ruined! It is ironic that, as a perfectionist who sets extremely high, inflexible goals, I am unfortunately setting goals that are often unreachable. It's almost as if I'm setting myself up for failure!

6 *Self-sabotage.*

Have you ever decided not to apply for a job or request a promotion or raise because you felt like you weren't qualified? I often deny myself a career opportunity before I even try because of this looming self-doubt and a fear of rejection. I probably set the bar higher than do the people actually hiring for the roles themselves! I self-sabotage because my inflexible goals of perfection and my intense fear of failure are debilitating. Has this ever happened to you?

7 *Typically turn down help.*

Especially when I'm new in a role, I want people to know that they made the right decision in choosing me. So, when they ask if I need any help, I confidently say, "No, I'm good!" I don't want them to think that they made a mistake. So, even though I actually *could* use help, I choose the more difficult path of trying to figure it out for myself. When people offer you help, do you accept it graciously, or do you turn them down?

8 *Overtly confident, covertly hiding low self-confidence.*

Do you ever tell folks, "I got this!" when in fact you feel like you have no idea what you're doing? I often pretend that I have everything covered, that I'm good at whatever the task is, when in fact it's a complete front. Have you ever felt this way?

Whether you have experienced just one of these symptoms or all eight of them at some point in your life, I want you to know that these feelings didn't come about in a vacuum.

Why Do We Experience Imposter Syndrome?

Many circumstances contribute to our self-doubt. As Black people living in America, we experience microaggressions almost daily, and many of them make us question ourselves. I remember, during my first week at a new job, my boss pulled me aside to have a private chat. He closed the door behind him and said, "I just want you to know that I didn't hire you because you're Black." It had never crossed my mind that I was hired for my skin color as opposed to my qualifications. Although I brushed it off in the moment, of course it made me wonder. Was he saying this to cover up the fact that he really did? Was this the *only* reason he'd hired me?

A friend of mine started a new job, and as she was walking down the hallway on her first day someone said to her, "Are you the new diversity hire?" She had an MBA from Stanford and her résumé was stellar, but that simple question would haunt her as she wondered if others thought of her merely as the "diversity hire," rather than as a valuable contributor to the organization.

We often experience imposter syndrome during moments of success. Have you ever started a new job, or received an award or promotion, and then wondered, *Did I really deserve it? Did they make a mistake?* Sometimes in these moments of success we might look around and realize that we are the only Black person to have this job/award/promotion/etc. *Did they give it to me just because I'm Black?*

Sometimes the way our colleagues treat us causes us to doubt ourselves. According to a recent Gallup survey, Black people are five times more likely than white people to have been treated as if they aren't smart. We also experience people acting like they are better than us at a rate three times as often. When your boss or your colleagues question your competence, you may begin to question your own competence as well.

Imposter syndrome also comes into play in the context of salaries and other compensation. Have you ever found out that your white colleague with the exact same title as you was being paid significantly more? When that happened to me, I started to associate my compensation with my self-worth, which was terrible for my mental health.

Jackson Gruver, a data analyst at compensation data and software firm PayScale, reported that "even as black or African American men climb the corporate ladder, they still make less than equally qualified white men." A PayScale study showed that "on average Black men earned 87 cents for every dollar a white man earned." For high-wage roles like lawyers, engineers, and doctors, Black women experience an even greater disparity in pay of 63 cents for every dollar a white man earns. Of course we are going to experience self-doubt if we look at the numbers and wonder whether our compensation is a reflection of our abilities.

I want you to know that if you have experienced imposter syndrome, you are not alone! Seventy percent of Americans experience imposter syndrome as well! Some of the most successful people admit that they, too, have self-doubt. Don Cheadle, Academy Award nominee and Golden Globe recipient, said, "All I can see is everything I'm doing wrong that is a sham and a fraud." He's starred in too many movies to count. He's an amazing actor, and yet he also feels like he's a fraud. I was incredibly surprised to hear that Michelle Obama is part of this 70 percent as well. "I still have a little imposter syndrome, it never goes away," she said. Michelle Obama! I share all this to give you some comfort in knowing that most of us will experience this, and you can still be a successful and fulfilled human being regardless of these feelings.

So, how do we get over it?

WEBAV for Imposter Syndrome

Mindfulness tools have been instrumental in helping me to counter imposter syndrome, and it requires a certain amount of courage to face imposter syndrome head-on. I want to share a framework called WEBAV, which I've developed over the years to build up my confidence and get me through the hardest moments of self-doubt.

WEBAV is an acronym that stands for:

Welcoming the Voice
Evidence Gathering
Breathwork
Affirmations
Visualization

I'm going to walk you through each one, and I invite you to do these practices as I describe them.

Welcoming the Voice

When we experience imposter syndrome, there is a voice in our head that is a source of negative commentary and criticism. When I hear the voice, I usually have one of two very extreme reactions. Either I try to shush it and ignore it or I get sucked into every word, believing that I'm going to do a bad job, that I'm not smart enough, strong enough, or capable enough to handle whatever is happening at the moment. Neither of these approaches ends well.

Instead I have found that taking the time to really get to know this voice has been most effective at overcoming it. Sun Tzu, in *The Art of War*, said:

> **If you know the enemy and know yourself, you need not fear the result of a hundred battles.**

The enemy in this case is the imposter-syndrome voice—this critic that has only negative things to say about you. So, how can we get to know this voice?

Whenever you hear this voice creep into your head, take a moment to allow it to speak, and listen as an outside observer. Put on some relaxing music. Close your eyes, and listen. Listen and take note of what this voice sounds like. Is it a high-pitched voice or a low-pitched voice? Does the voice have a gender? What is the tone the voice is using? Is it sarcastic, critical, condescending, or mean? And what is this voice saying to you?

At one job, every day I went to work thinking I would get fired. This imposter-syndrome voice drilled this into my head every single day. So, one day I sat down, closed my eyes, and let the voice have the floor. I listened, and this is what I heard. A British man with an authoritative tone was sternly berating me. With his strong accent, he told me that, no matter how hard I tried, I was going to get fired. He told me that I wasn't going to meet the sales goals our CEO was expecting from me. He told me that I didn't have enough experience for the job, and that all my colleagues were going to realize this and get rid of me. As I was listening, I thought, *If I were to give this voice a name, what would it be?* Immediately I knew that this British man's name was Bob!

It is not lost on me that a British man with an authoritative tone might somehow be related to my own ancestral and generational trauma. My Jamaican ancestors were under British rule, and slavery was just as real there as it was in the United States. However, there was something powerful about giving Bob a name, and recognizing that I am not Bob, and that Bob only lives inside my head. I wrote down all the things that Bob said, and the mere act of doing this created a sort of separation between me and Bob's words.

Although this example was about work, I hear this voice about so many things in my life, from how romances are going to pan out to whether I'll be able to survive a day of rock climbing in one piece.

Take a moment to think about a time when you experienced self-doubt, when this imposter-syndrome voice started creeping into your mind. Close your eyes and imagine this voice. If you were to give this voice a name, what would it be? Write down all the things this voice says.

"You're going to get fired!"

Evidence That Supports

- Another Black woman was fired
- Implicit bias/racism at work is real
- Potential layoffs

Evidence That Disproves

- I got top-rated performance reviews
- I exceeded my annual goals
- Colleagues tell me I'm doing a great job
- I'm being given more responsibility
- I was promoted last year

*E*vidence Gathering

In Clance and Imes's definition of imposter syndrome, they explain that we experience these thoughts of self-doubt "despite evidence of high achievement." More often than not, our imposter-syndrome voice does not have an objective and evidence-based perspective. It is incredibly powerful to ground your acceptance or rejection of your imposter-syndrome voice's statements in evidence and facts. If someone made a claim to you that had no evidence backing it up, would you believe them? Why should this be any different?

This is the approach that I took with Bob, my British compadre who never had anything good to say. I looked at all the things that he said and chose the statement that I found most triggering, that kept coming up over and over again. At that time it was, *You're going to get fired!* Every time I would hear it, I would get stressed out with so much fear that it was going to happen that very day. I would arrive at work completely on edge.

I got a piece of paper and wrote "You're going to get fired!" at the top of the page. I drew a vertical line down the middle of the page to make two columns. On the left side, I listed the evidence that supported this statement. As I thought about it, there weren't too many things I could add that were actual facts or evidence. There was another Black woman in the office who'd been fired, so that was definitely on the list. Did her getting fired mean that I would? I couldn't be sure, but it was on my mind a lot, so I added it. Racism is real, and I couldn't necessarily trust my colleagues to be aware of their biases! I also added that the company's financial performance hadn't been great, so that could lead to layoffs. In this case it wouldn't be me alone losing my job, but still, I added it to the list. I couldn't come up with any facts about my performance that supported this statement, though.

In the right column, I made a list of all the evidence that disproved this statement. This was hard at first, because I'm not the best at self-praise. I usually just focus on the negative. So, I tried to think about what others might contribute to this list: my colleagues, my friends, and people who know me well. Then it was a lot easier. I listed all the big clients whom I had already brought into the company. I listed the revenue numbers for my team to date, which looked pretty impressive. I wrote down positive feedback that I had received in performance reviews. When I was finished, I realized that the list in the right column was significantly longer! Why was I spending so much time worrying about something that had so much evidence against it?

Take a look at the list of statements your imposter-syndrome voice said in the "Welcoming the Voice" section. Circle the statement that comes up the most often and is most triggering. Write that statement at the top of a piece of paper, and draw a line down the middle to make two columns so that you can list facts and evidence that support it on the left side and facts and evidence that disprove it on the right. Once you're finished, take a moment to reflect on your lists. Are they all truly facts and evidence? How long are your lists relative to each other? What would your biggest fans add to the list of evidence disproving the statement? Notice how you feel as you read these lists.

Breathwork

Sometimes the imposter-syndrome voice can be all-consuming. The critic's commentary repeats itself so much that it's distracting! When I was worrying every day that I would get fired, I realized that I needed some serious grounding, and I used to practice the Solar Plexus Breath before I left my house in the morning. This simple technique helped me stay calm so that when I arrived at work I would be able to jump right into the day.

In the chakra system, the network of energy channels in your body described in chapter 6, the solar plexus is the chakra in the abdomen. It lies above the belly button, up to the breastbone. This chakra is the center of our self-confidence, our willpower, and our ability to take action. Intentional breathing into this area can be very effective at helping us believe in ourselves and giving us that extra internal push to do whatever we are hesitant to do.

I used to wake up thinking, *Is today going to be the day? Are they going to realize that I shouldn't be in this job? Is my boss going to replace me with some young white tech bro he went kiteboarding or cycling with over the weekend?* I couldn't let this be the dominant force in my psyche. So, before leaving my house in the morning, I practiced the Solar Plexus Breath. If you have days like this, here's what you can do.

Take a few minutes to sit in a quiet place. If you sit in a chair, make sure that both of your feet are placed firmly on the ground. If you sit on the floor, make sure that you are in a position that is comfortable for your knees. Regardless of where you sit, be conscious that you don't slouch and that your back is straight so that you can maximize oxygen flow. With one hand at each side, place your fingers below your rib cage, and curl your thumbs around your back. Take a deep breath into this area, and feel the air push your fingers forward in the front and your thumbs out in back. Inhale slowly for a count of four, ensuring that you breathe equally into the front and the back. Exhale slowly for a count of four, feeling your fingers and your thumbs come back in toward the center. Repeat this breath, in for one-two-three-four, out for one-two-three-four, feeling your fingers and thumbs move with the breath, for five long, deep, breaths. At the end, say to yourself, "You got this!" or any other phrase of positive reinforcement that works for you. After this short breathing exercise, I'm ready. I can begin my day with a clear mind.

Although the Solar Plexus Breath is helpful for general grounding and to find our self-confidence, there are other helpful breathing techniques for specific situations in which imposter syndrome plays a role. Have you ever had a hard time focusing on a project because you were worried that you wouldn't do a good job, or your track record in that area didn't make you feel like you could do it? The Humming Bee Breath in chapter 3 could be your answer. I used to joke that it was my version of Adderall when I needed to get work done that my brain just resisted. For me, one of the hardest things to concentrate on is contracts. I always feel like I am bad at it, that legal documents just aren't my thing. Whenever I have to sit down and read the details, my brain just glosses over the words, and I have to read the same sentence over and over again just to understand it. Before I start a task like this, I sit

Solar Plexus Breath

Inhale . . . 1–2–3–4

Exhale . . . 4–3–2–1

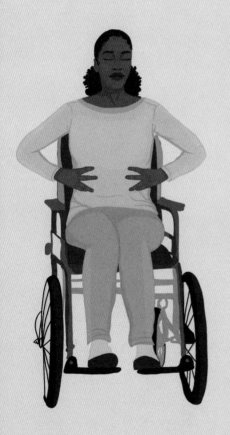
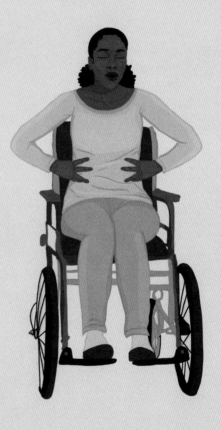

down, plug my ears with my thumbs, cover my eyes with my fingers, and take five to ten deep breaths, humming on each exhalation. When I open my eyes, my brain is ready. I'm completely focused and I can actually pay attention. I also use this technique when I'm going to sit down to create something, whether it's a mindfulness training class plan or new music. It allows me to go all in when I start. No distractions.

Another instance where breathwork has been helpful for me is when I'm about to give a presentation. I get overwhelmed with what-ifs—*What if I mess up? What if they don't like me? What if they ask me a question I can't answer?* In these situations, I go to the bathroom wherever I am, and I do the Lion's Breath described in chapter 6. I bring my arms up like a goalpost, inhale deeply, and then exhale, sticking my tongue out as far as possible and making an audible animal-like sound. I like to do this in the mirror because then something clicks in my brain that gives me that extra oomph to believe that I can do it. After a few of these in the mirror, I walk into the meeting with a wild confidence that is unstoppable and fierce! The next time you have to give a speech or presentation, I invite you to try the Lion's Breath before walking into the room. Yes, it looks crazy, but you can try it in the privacy of a bathroom or somewhere else out of sight. The results will definitely surprise you.

Let's say that you didn't have time to do any breathing techniques before speaking. Your heart starts racing, and you feel sweat pouring from your armpits. This happened to me when I was giving a speech at a big conference. The hall was filled with people. The spotlight was on me, and suddenly I was overwhelmed by the fact that all these people were much older than I and predominately white. I felt myself shaking, and I was already up at the podium. All eyes were on me, and I was sweating up a storm! This was clearly my fight-or-flight-or-freeze response in full force. I needed to calm my nervous system ASAP! At this moment, I did the Belly Breath described in chapter 4. I breathed deeply, expanding my belly as much as possible when I inhaled, and brought my belly back to my spine very intentionally when I exhaled. Just one or two of these in the moments before I started speaking, and during any of the pauses between slides, were life-changing. I was able to get in the groove, and I ended up getting a lot of praise afterward! If this ever happens to you in the moment and you are having all sorts of nervous feelings about what people are thinking and how you are going to do, just try a couple of deep Belly Breaths.

Affirmations

I used to think that affirmations were a cheesy self-help thing. I wrote them off as not for me. I would think of *Saturday Night Live*'s Stuart Smalley and his comedic catchphrase "I'm good enough, I'm smart enough, and doggone it, people like me!" I didn't think they actually worked! However, at one point in my life, my self-doubt became so overwhelming that I was willing to try anything. I did my due diligence into how they work and their effectiveness, and I was very surprised. Research shows that using affirmations before a high-pressure meeting can improve your confidence, calm your nervous system, and increase the probability of a successful outcome.

So, how do you come up with an affirmation? First of all, affirmations should be in the present tense. They often can turn a negative into a positive. For example, if you typically say, "I'm not smart enough to get promoted," you might turn it around and say, "I'm a skilled and experienced financial analyst." Research also shows that the simple act of adding your name to a positive affirmation can have a powerful effect on how you perceive yourself. Using your name rather than *I* allows for some distancing from the statement. This separation allows your ego to get out of the way and the statement to seem less personal, and therefore less stressful and emotional.

Here's an example of an insecurity that I've had in my musical life. I was trained as a classical violinist under the Suzuki method, which focuses on listening to a piece and playing it exactly as you heard it. It involves reading music that was already written for you to perform. In the past ten years, I've started playing more contemporary music like hip-hop, rock, and folk, with live bands. This means that I have to improvise on the spot. There's no sheet music to tell me what to do, and in a live show, anything can happen, so improvisation is key. My classical training left me feeling very inadequate around this skill. So, I wrote an affirmation about it:

Zee is amazing at violin improv!

It says "Zee" instead of "I." It's present tense. Zee *is*. It's not some future state, a wish for something I hope to be. It is the case right now. I turned a negative, which in my mind was that I'm terrible at improv, into a positive. I'm amazing at it! It's also short enough that I can remember it and repeat it easily.

Take a moment to think about what your affirmation might be. Think of an area of your life in which you experience a lot of self-doubt, and write your own affirmation about it. Remember, make it present tense and use your name!

Once you have your affirmation, what should you do with it? If you write it down once and never look at it again, it won't have any impact. The power lies in repeating it to yourself throughout the day. You might consider putting it on your calendar at regular intervals to remind you of it. Something happens in your brain the more you engage with this thought. It solidifies like a learned behavior and you actually start to believe it. The concept of neuroplasticity is your brain's ability to reorganize itself by forming new neural connections. This means that you are capable of learning and changing your beliefs and thought patterns. It's also helpful to repeat your affirmation as soon as a negative thought or self-doubt comes into your mind. Your mindfulness practice will allow you to recognize that this imposter-syndrome voice has arrived, and you have the power to reply with your affirmation!

I have found two practices involving affirmations to be incredibly impactful. The first is to repeat your affirmation in the mirror. This can be a bit jarring at first, because we rarely spend time in the mirror talking to ourselves. So, if you try it once and are feeling uncomfortable, be patient with yourself and try it a few more times. This is how to do it. Look into your eyes. Don't get distracted by judging yourself. It's not about your hair, some new wrinkles, or what you look like. Try to push aside any temptation to assess your appearance. Instead, focus on looking into your eyes in the mirror, as if you're talking to someone you love, and say your affirmation ten times. Say it with feeling and with intention. I find it easier to do this if I change which words I emphasize each time and count to keep track. For example:

> **ZEE** is amazing at violin improv . . . one.
> Zee **IS** amazing at violin improv . . . two.
> Zee is **AMAZING** at violin improv . . . three.
> Zee is amazing at **VIOLIN** improv . . . four.

Try this, and see how you feel!

I also find it really powerful to accompany my affirmations with a physical posture that helps me really own the statement. Stand up, with your feet a little wider than hip width apart. Bring your arms out to your sides parallel to the floor, stick your chest out, and yell your affirmation with a bold tone that screams "I believe this wholeheartedly!" Repeat your affirmation ten times, counting, and changing the emphasized word each time. Remember to be loud and be bold!

Visualization

Why visualization? We stimulate the same regions of the brain when we visualize an action as we do when we actually perform that same action. This is why Olympic athletes use visualization as part of their training. Research shows that it can improve performance by as much as 45 percent! The opposite is also true. If our imposter-syndrome voice takes over, we might start visualizing a big failure and that might become a self-fulfilling prophecy. So, how do you even begin to visualize something? There is extensive literature on the

subject and no one way to do it, but I will share with you what works for me.

First, find yourself a quiet place where no one will disturb you. Turn on some peaceful meditative music to allow your mind to settle. Set a timer so that you won't be distracted by watching the clock and how long you've been doing this. I suggest anywhere from three to ten minutes if you're just starting out. Close your eyes and take three deep breaths. Think about a specific event or scenario that you want to do well in. Be as specific as possible. For me, violin performances can be a nightmare for my nerves, so before a show I do a visualization exercise for that specific show. Once you have a specific situation in mind that you want to succeed in, imagine yourself sitting in a movie theater watching a blank, white screen. Slowly allow images to appear on the screen depicting the situation you are thinking of. See yourself on the screen, performing at your very best. Notice all the details. Where are you? What do you see? What do you hear? What are you doing? What are you wearing? What are you saying? Whom are you with? What is the expression on their faces? Imagine everything happening exactly as you want it to happen.

Now imagine that you are not watching the movie but are in it. It is all happening to you and around you. Look at your surroundings. Feel yourself engaging with the environment. If you're speaking, hear yourself talk. If you're doing something physical, feel the muscles in your body doing what you're doing. Feel yourself performing at your very best! Allow yourself to bathe in the experience, creating it and feeling it into being. Trust and know that it is happening, and enjoy it! When the timer goes off, inhale deeply, exhale, and open your eyes.

The more you visualize something, the more your brain experiences knowing and feeling what it's like to make it happen, so I invite you to give it a try!

Key Points to Remember

- If you have experienced imposter syndrome, remember that you are not alone! Seventy percent of Americans, including some very famous and accomplished individuals, have also experienced it.

- The imposter-syndrome voice will come and go; however, it's important to be mindful of when it does arise so that you can counter it with one or all of the tools in WEBAV!

- The breathwork techniques mentioned in prior chapters can be very effective in countering imposter syndrome as well: Humming Bee Breath is great for focus and concentration. Lion's Breath is powerful before you need to give a speech or present in a meeting. Belly Breath can calm you down when you're in the moment and freaking out inside.

Mindfulness Practice Toolkit

Mindfulness Practice 25: Welcoming the Voice

When you hear your imposter-syndrome voice start making negative commentary in your head:

1 Take a moment to pause.

2 Set a timer for two to five minutes.

3 Turn on some relaxing music.

4 Close your eyes and take a deep breath.

5 Listen to the voice.

6 Pay attention to what the voice sounds like. What sort of pitch does it have? What sort of tone is it using? What specific things is it saying to you?

7 If you were to give this voice a name, what would it be?

8 When the timer goes off, open your eyes and write down all the things that the voice says.

Mindfulness Practice 26: Evidence Gathering

When you have a list of statements that your imposter-syndrome voice says about you:

1 Look at the list of statements, choose one that comes up often, and circle it.

2 Write this statement at the top of a piece of paper.

3 Draw a line down the middle of the page below the statement to create two columns.

4 Set a timer for three to five minutes.

5 In the left-hand column, make a list of all the facts and evidence that support the statement.

6 In the right-hand column, make a list of all the facts and evidence that disprove the statement.

7 When you're finished, bring to mind someone who is your biggest fan. What would they add to your lists?

8 Take a minute to read your two lists, and notice how you feel.

Mindfulness Practice 27: Solar Plexus Breath

When your imposter-syndrome voice is so distracting that you need some grounding:

1 Find a quiet place to sit.

2 If you are in a chair, be sure that both feet are placed firmly on the ground. If you are on the floor, be sure that your position is comfortable for your knees.

3 Sit with your back straight to maximize oxygen flow.

4 With one hand at each side, place your fingers below your rib cage and curl your thumbs around your back.

5 Inhale deeply into this area, feeling the air push your fingers forward in the front and your thumbs out in the back.

6 Inhale slowly for a count of four, ensuring you are breathing equally into the front and the back.

7 Exhale slowly for a count of four, feeling your fingers and thumbs come back toward the center.

8 Repeat for five long, deep breaths.

Mindfulness Practice 28: Affirmations

When your brain could use some rewiring to get rid of negative thought patterns:

1 Think of an area of your life in which you experienced a lot of self-doubt.

2 Write an affirmation about this area.

3 Use the present tense.

4 Consider turning a negative statement from your imposter-syndrome voice into a positive statement.

5 Use your name instead of *I*.

6 Be sure your affirmation is short enough that you can repeat it and remember it easily.

7 Put the affirmation in your calendar so that it comes up as a notification and reminder.

8 Repeat your affirmation in the mirror.

    a Try to push aside any temptation to assess your appearance.

    b Look into your own eyes.

    c Say your affirmation ten times, with feeling and with intention.

    d Change which words you emphasize each time, and count to keep track.

9 If mirror work doesn't feel right, try steps 8c and 8d, with the following physical posture:

   a Stand up, with your feet a little wider than hip width apart.

   b Bring your arms out to your sides parallel to the floor, stick your chest out.

   c Yell your affirmation in a bold tone that screams "I believe this wholeheartedly!"

Mindfulness Practice 29: Visualization

When there is a specific event or situation that you would like to do well in:

1 Find yourself a quiet place where no one will disturb you, and turn on some peaceful meditative music.

2 Set a timer for an interval that feels right for you (three to ten minutes if you are new to this).

3 Close your eyes and take three deep breaths.

4 Think about a specific event or scenario that you want to do well in. Be as specific as possible.

5 Imagine yourself sitting in a movie theater watching a blank, white screen. Slowly allow images to appear on the screen that depict the situation that you are thinking of. See yourself on the screen, performing at your very best and notice all the details.

6 Now imagine that you are not watching the movie but are in it. Look at your surroundings and feel yourself engaging with the environment and doing and feeling everything as if you were right there, right now.

7 Allow yourself to bathe in the experience, creating it and feeling it into being.

8 When the timer goes off, inhale deeply, then exhale, and open your eyes.

CHAPTER TEN

To Code-Switch or Not to Code-Switch?

Many years ago, a young Black woman asked for my advice on how to rise through the ranks at our company. She was the receptionist, I was in a leadership position, and we were the only Black women at the time. She wanted to transition into a project-management role and was facing difficulties convincing our white colleagues to believe in her. She was smart, she was motivated, and she was hardworking. However, it felt like she could do nothing right in their eyes. I told her what I had always been told about how to survive in white spaces.

"You have to play their game," I said. "Play by their rules." I told her that she should consider being more intentional about speaking in their vernacular and dressing in a more "professional" manner. I told her that she needed to go above and beyond in everything that she did, because we needed to be overqualified before they would consider us for anything. She took my advice, and, although our colleagues started to notice and make comments about how her performance had improved, she was not happy. She couldn't be herself, and the act was draining.

They never offered her the opportunity to transition into another role, and she left the company for spaces that actually valued her and believed in her. Today, with her natural hair, bright yellow suits, and hot pink acrylic nails, she is running her own venture-capital fund.

I started to wonder if I had given her bad advice. We can offer feedback based only on our own experiences. When I was in high school and college, I participated in several programs focused on developing talented young minorities such as INROADS and LEAD. There are many programs like this out there, and I am forever grateful because they introduced me to the business world, they offered me opportunities for internships, and I wouldn't be where I am today without them. In these programs, I learned that to be successful I had to be "professional," and they were very specific about what that meant. Speak the way *they* speak. Straight hair. Suits or business-casual outfits that are not too form-fitting, with skirts that always fall below the knee. Nothing that could be deemed provocative or sexy in any way. At business dinners, no elbows on the table. Use the right fork during the right course. A friend of mine who also participated in these programs describes *professionalism* as "the biggest white-supremacy scam ever, just a passive-aggressive form of oppression." Whether you agree with her or not, you can't deny that some people are labeled "unprofessional" based on the way they present themselves, and this can have an impact on how they are treated and the opportunities that are given to them.

I shared with my colleague what I had learned from observing Black professionals that had "made it," and the things that I did in order to progress in my career. I used the harshest of chemicals on my hair. I left my Washington, D.C., slang at home. I did everything I could to make them feel like I was one of them. I dressed the way they dressed. I pretended to like what they liked. Before I knew it, there were two versions of me, the "work" me and the "real" me. Do you ever feel this way?

A Trinidadian friend who worked at McKinsey, a prestigious management-consulting firm, shared that when he was going to a work holiday party his wife asked him, "Are you bringing your McKinsey self or your Carnival self?" His McKinsey self was very serious and buttoned up. His Carnival self was fun-loving, made jokes, and enjoyed music and dancing. It was a work event, so can you guess what his answer was?

Code-Switching Defined

Do you ever feel like you adjust what you share and how you communicate when you are in white spaces? *Merriam-Webster's Dictionary* defines *code-switching* as "the switching from the linguistic system of one language or dialect to that of another." This definition is very much limited to speech and language. In *Language and Interracial Communication in the United States: Speaking in Black and White,* George B. Ray describes African American code-switching as "a skill that holds benefits in relation to the way success is often measured in institutional and professional settings." Ray's definition gets into the reasons why we code-switch, which I will soon dive into because there are many more. And he describes it as a skill. In my experience, this skill goes way beyond language. It is about how we present ourselves in every way.

More than the words themselves, even the volume and our tone can be perceived as threatening. In fact, one friend said that everything he does in white spaces is so that he can be seen as a "nonthreatening person of color." I can relate, because I'm forever paranoid about being viewed as an "angry Black woman."

Even nonverbal cues can play a role in how we're perceived. Have you ever found yourself conscious of your facial expressions? I'm someone who doesn't need to say anything and you can tell exactly what I'm thinking, so I started honing the skill of hiding it. Sometimes I would go to work events and my cheek muscles would be exhausted from the fake smiling. In white spaces, we feel pressure to make people feel comfortable, so we smile, smile, smile! In the Mary J. Blige documentary *My Life,* she describes how smiling while walking down the street was actually detrimental to her safety and survival in her neighborhood.

I felt this way when I was growing up as well, so smiling like this did not come naturally to me. In my early days, people said I had "resting bitch face." My friend describes her own as "resting skeptic face." Whatever you might want to call it, in my experience it doesn't bode well in predominantly white spaces.

Code-switching is more than what we say and how we say it; it's also what we don't say. I used to hide my socioeconomic background. I remember how nervous I was when I "came out" as a poor person. I was working at an education start-up and I started a scholarship program for those in need. When our chief marketing officer told me that it was a waste of time and that she didn't see the point of scholarships, I felt the need to explain not just to her but to the world why it was important. I wrote a blog post exposing my own circumstances as a child, the drive-by shootings in my neighborhood, the financial struggles of my family, and how scholarships changed my life. When I pushed the Publish button, my heart rate shot up because I was so scared that removing this one mask might change the way my colleagues viewed me. Would they no longer respect me? Would they pity me? Was I putting my job in danger by sharing that their world of Teslas and luxury vacations was completely foreign to me and my upbringing?

These masks we wear are real. I have hidden basic things about myself like my culture and how I grew up, and even how I spent my weekend, my hobbies, and my real opinions and views. A client once told me that she went to a trap yoga event over the weekend, but, when her colleagues asked her what she did, she said she didn't do much. Why? She didn't want to have to explain what trap music was, and she didn't want to highlight how she was different.

When you get into political views, the conversation can get pretty charged, and depending on my energy level I might choose to not engage and share what I really think because I don't want to put myself in a situation where I'll get upset and triggered. Sometimes I even refrain from using the word *white* with white people because I don't want to hurt their feelings. Many liberal white people don't want to be called white because it's associated with the actions of their ancestors and of white supremacists today. So, I'll choose to avoid the word *white* to ensure their comfort.

Why Do We Code-Switch?

"Making white people comfortable is the most important thing in getting ahead in this world."

This is what a Black woman who I love and respect said when I asked her why she code-switches. I cringed when I heard it, and it made me sad that this is what many of us have been taught and believe.

Do you code-switch? If so, why and when? Below are ten reasons that I, and people that I know, code-switch. As you read them, I invite you to consider which ones ring true for you, and perhaps create your own list.

1 Code-switching could save my life. Doctors might provide me with better medical treatment. The police might have a lower likelihood of abusing their power.

2 I do it to fit in! I don't want to be seen and treated as "other."

3 My colleagues will think I'm more "professional."

4 It increases my ability to progress in my career, get better jobs, and ultimately increase my compensation.

5 People will respect me more. If I don't code-switch, they will make judgments about my education and intelligence.

6 Because I'm the only Black person here, it's my duty to represent my people as best I can, because people will judge other Black people they meet based on how I act.

7 To get my point across. I don't want to be misunderstood because of my language choices.

8 It helps me get what I want. If I'm at a store, they'll treat me better. In an interview, I'll get the job. As a waiter, I'll get better tips. In a sales meeting, I'll close the deal.

9 To avoid microaggressions. It's already an unsafe environment because they judge me before I even open my mouth, so this is a defense mechanism. I don't want their questions or their comments.

10 Black people that I look up to and admire code-switch. Look at how Obama gives dap or a handshake depending on whom he's interacting with!

The Costs of Code-Switching

Although there are many reasons that we code-switch, we rarely talk about the impact that code-switching has on us. One day, I got home from work completely depleted. I plopped down on the couch and I could barely move my body. My mind felt like a pile of mush, and I didn't want to do anything. Even turning on mindless TV felt like too much. I thought I would sleep it off, but the next morning nothing had changed. My calendar was filled with meetings, and I didn't have any more to give. I just couldn't. I called in sick, which was a rare thing for me, because I was trained that unless you're absolutely dying, you go to school, you go to work, and you handle your business. But on this particular morning there was no decision to be made. My mind and my body made it for me. I canceled everything to do the one thing that we Black women rarely allow ourselves to do. Rest.

At that time, I hadn't had much exposure to the concept of burnout. However, as I look back, that is exactly what happened to me. The amount of energy that I had to expend to fit into their world, on top of an already large workload, snowballed into more than I could handle. A *Harvard Business Review* article, "The Costs of Code-Switching," explains that, in addition to burnout, "seeking to avoid stereotypes is hard work, and can deplete cognitive resources and hinder performance." We are using so much of our brainpower on code-switching that it's taking away our focus from the actual job at hand! Have you ever felt this way?

In addition to exhaustion and burnout, code-switching has definitely put a dent in my self-esteem and my sense of self-worth over the years. As I chose the version of me that conformed to what the majority deemed professional, I sometimes found myself being embarrassed or ashamed of the raw, unadulterated version of me. W. E. B. DuBois, in *The Souls of Black Folk,* describes our experiences in a way that really resonates with me:

> It is a peculiar sensation, this double-consciousness, this sense of always looking at one's self through the eyes of others, of measuring one's soul by the tape of a world that looks on in amused contempt and pity. One ever feels his two-ness, an American, a Negro; two souls, two thoughts, two unreconciled strivings; two warring ideals in one dark body, whose dogged strength alone keeps it from being torn asunder.

This concept of "warring ideals" plagued me, because one of those ideals was winning for the majority of the hours that I was awake. And if I was choosing other people's version of me, what did that imply about the version that was true to me? It's been a long journey to come to the point of truly loving myself, loving every part of myself. Code-switching has made that a challenging journey, and why shouldn't we be proud of who we are in our entirety?

To Code-Switch or Not to Code-Switch? That Is the Question

Some people have decided they are done with code-switching. A friend of mine said, "I do what I want, where I want, around whom I want, wherever I am in the world. *Basta!* (Enough!)" Some believe that sharing who we really are and bringing our whole selves actually makes us better at our jobs! Former Netflix chief marketing officer Bozoma Saint

John, during an "Anatomy of a Badass" session at Harvard Business School, shared the following:

> I know, I know for sure, that I am a much more powerful execu-
> tive because I am a "sort of" immigrant. . . . I am a much better
> executive because I'm a single mom to an eleven-year-old girl. I'm
> a much better executive because I'm a widow. I'm a much better
> executive because I can twerk like it's nobody's business . . . and
> therefore I don't hide them. I bring them. Full display! I use them
> to influence everything that I do. And here is the center of it. It is
> important. Our individual experiences are important. They mat-
> ter. They count!

However, there are others who see code-switching as a skill and an asset. A friend from both college and business school said, "For me it's tailoring your message to your audience. If I meet an Italian, I will speak Italian. If I meet someone from Harvard, I will ask what house they were in or reference some other shared element of culture. Definitely I see it as an advantage to have the dexterity to navigate other cultures effec-tively." Another friend says that she sees it as "meeting people where they are."

I'm not going to tell you to code-switch or not to code-switch. Instead I invite you to take a mindful approach to this decision. There was a moment in my life when I realized that I was on autopilot. I assumed that I *had* to code-switch in any and every white space. This is the opposite of mindfulness. I was lacking any sort of awareness of my actions, and there was no intention behind it.

I want to share with you a practice that helped me on my jour-ney to being intentional about code-switching. It's called "The Work," developed by speaker and author Byron Katie. She describes it as four questions that allow you to access the wisdom that always exists within you. It starts with a belief. In the context of code-switching, what belief do you have that causes you to code-switch? Put differently, what do you believe will happen if you don't code-switch? Choose a belief that stands out the most for you.

The first question is, "Is it true?" My belief was that if I didn't code-switch, I wouldn't be able to advance in my career. So, I asked myself, "Is it true?" My gut response was *Of course it's true. That's why I've been code-switching all of my life!* When you consider your own belief, what's your answer?

If you answered no, you can skip to the third question. However, if you answered yes, then let's move on to **the second question, "Can you absolutely know that it's true?"** For me, I can't absolutely *know* know. But I definitely think so. Racism has been around for a long time. The leadership-development programs for minorities that I attended twenty years ago told me so! But what if things have changed since then? I guess my answer is that I can't be 100 percent sure. What about you? Can you absolutely know that your belief is true? Pause and think about it.

The third question is, "How do you react, what happens, when you believe that thought?" For me, I get really sad that this is the state of America. I put up a lot of walls because I feel like I need to protect myself. I'm in a constant state of paranoia about exposing too much. I get anxious and scared that I won't achieve my goals, and that maybe my company will find some arbitrary reason to fire me. The thoughts are like a broken record. *I'm gonna get fired. I'm gonna get fired.* This added stress makes me actually perform worse at work because I'm so nervous, then I beat myself up about it; it's a vicious cycle. This need to be performing all the time is exhausting, and, as I shared earlier, burnout is real!

What about you? How do you react; what happens when you believe that thought? What emotions arise? What images of the past and future do you see when you believe the thought? How do you treat yourself and others when you believe the thought? Take a moment to write down your answers. Find a quiet space and think about it. Be honest with yourself.

The fourth question is, "Who would you be without that thought?" Really think about this. Close your eyes and think about who you would be without this thought. If I didn't think my career would be hindered by being my true self at work, I would feel free. Instead of feeling like I was walking on eggshells or having to watch my back, I would feel more natural. I would have the confidence to say what I actually thought. I would really, really shine. Maybe I'd even be happy as I did my job. I would treat myself better. I would treat others better as well.

What about you? Take a moment and write down who you would be without this thought. Once you feel like you've said all you need to say, read what you wrote. Sit with it. How does it make you feel?

Now that we've walked through the four questions, **there is one final step: Turn it around.** I found this step to be the hardest to grasp, and having lots of examples really helped. In this step, we explore turning the thought around and observing how each turnaround changes the way that we feel and our understanding of the situation. What do I mean by turning it around? Think about different versions of the opposite of the belief statement. If my original belief was that being my true self at work is going to hinder my career, here are a few ways to turn it around.

The simplest is just to say the direct opposite of the statement: "Being my true self at work is *not* going to hinder my career." The first time I said that out loud, it gave me a sense of comfort. I took a deep breath and wondered, *Could this* actually *be true?*

Another way to turn it around is to change the actor, or subject, in the statement so that you have agency. For example, "I am hindering my career by not being my true self at work." Sitting with this turnaround made me wonder, *Am I self-sabotaging? Am I limiting myself and my own progress because of this belief?*

Here's another example of putting myself in the driver's seat with a turnaround:

"I am hindering my career by continuing to work at a place where I don't feel comfortable being myself." I can choose to quit! I would need to figure out my finances, but working here is a choice. This one was

huge for me because I was so used to feeling stuck. They didn't own me, and I have choices in this life.

Take a look at your original belief statement, and turn it around. Create as many turnaround statements as come to you. Once you're done, read each one and pause. How does it make you feel? What emotions come up? How does this change your perspective on the situation?

Going through these four questions and the turnarounds helped me see that my automatic code-switching wasn't necessary in all situations. Choosing to be intentional and mindful about your choice to code-switch is a powerful decision. There are many circumstances in which you might not have time to go through this exercise. Sometimes the decision to code-switch could mean life or death, like during a traffic stop by police. A good friend of mine had a stroke at age thirty-five, and she spends a lot of her time with older white doctors that determine her treatments, medications, and specialist referrals; these interactions and the doctor's choices have a huge impact on her life. She might get to the fourth question, "Who would you be without that thought?" and realize that in medical situations she wouldn't be alive without it.

I want to leave you with the fact that you have agency about when you code-switch and when you don't. If you choose to code-switch, you should know that you, all of you, are amazing! There is no one like you out there, and there are so many reasons to love you!

Key Points to Remember

- There are many reasons to code-switch, and some see it as an asset and a skill that can be helpful both in your career and in life.

- Code-switching can come with costs, including burnout, fatigue, and possible damages to your self-esteem.

- You have agency about when you code-switch and when you don't. If you are code-switching, consider whether you are doing it on autopilot, because others expect you to, or whether you are making a deliberate decision in that particular situation.

Mindfulness Practice Toolkit

Mindfulness Practice 30:
Byron Katie's "The Work": Four Questions

When considering whether to code-switch:

1 Identify the belief that is driving your reason for code-switching. What would happen if you didn't code-switch? Write it down. If there are multiple beliefs, circle the one that is most prominent in your mind.

2 In your journal, answer these four questions about your belief:

    a Is it true?

    b Can you absolutely know that it's true?

    c How do you react, what happens, when you believe that thought?

    d Who would you be without that thought?

3 Turn the belief statement around. Start by stating the opposite of the statement. Explore changing the subject, or actor, in the statement. Create as many turnaround statements as come to you. Once you're finished, read each one and pause. How does it make you feel? What emotions come up? How does this change your perspective on the situation?

CHAPTER ELEVEN

A Journey to Self-Love

You are your best thing.

—Toni Morrison

Being Black in America can be filled with a number of challenges, from racial profiling to microaggressions and so much more. Although many practices can help you get through them, the most important thing to remember throughout all of it is self-care and self-love. We can't control what other people do or say, but we can control all that is within.

Self-love has been a journey for me. It took me a long time to really, truly believe that I loved myself and that I was worthy of love. For the moments of exhaustion, shame, or self-hate, there is a writing exercise I want to share with you that helped me come back to my center and appreciate all the things that make me, me.

I invite you to set a timer for five minutes and answer this question in your journal:

What do I love about myself?

It might feel weird at first, and I'm always self-conscious about seeming arrogant, even in the privacy of my own mind. But I invite you to try it out. No one is going to read this but you. What do you love about yourself? Write the first things that come to mind. Don't think too hard about it. If it comes to you, write it down. It counts. It matters. If you can't come up with anything, just start writing anyway. The act of moving your pen and getting started, even if it's to write "I have no idea what I love about myself," will build momentum and get your ideas flowing. If you feel really stuck, think about what someone who loves you would say, and consider whether you agree with them. If so, write it down!

When I did this the first time, there were things on this list that people who know me might have also said. There were also things I wrote that I'm not sure many people even knew, because I'd never let them see that part of me. What comes up for you?

When the five minutes are up, take a moment to read what you wrote. Close your eyes and experience what it feels like to know and appreciate all the amazing things that are a part of you!

There are so many reasons to love yourself, and a critical component of self-love is self-care. We are exhausted from code-switching. We are exhausted from microaggressions. We are exhausted from the many challenges that come our way. To truly love ourselves, we must take care of ourselves. I have two suggestions for self-care that have been game-changers in my life.

Self-Care Practice 1:
Intentional Morning & Evening Routines

I used to be on autopilot, and I didn't realize how much of an impact my morning and evening practices had on my energy levels, my productivity, and my ability to feel good throughout my day. This is where mindfulness, yet again, was extremely helpful to me. Awareness of my current state was the first step. Let's start with morning routines. What do your typical mornings look like?

I used to wake up startled by my alarm clock and hit Snooze as many times as I could afford. My alarm was on my phone, and when I did wake up I couldn't help but look at my notifications. I might see a news article pop up and find myself succumbing to click bait and suddenly watching footage of something terrible that set the tone for my entire day. I might click on a work email and find myself responding, half awake, from my bed—not exactly the most articulate emails I've ever written. I often found myself caught in a mindless Instagram scrolling session, only to realize that twenty minutes had gone by and I was running late and needed to shower. This would lead to getting ready in a mad frenzy, skipping breakfast, or scarfing down something way too quickly for my digestion.

As for evening routines, I would be so exhausted from my workday that I would eat dinner and pour myself a very generous glass (or two or three) of red wine. I would turn on the television because my brain needed a rest, and the next thing I knew I had passed out on the couch with the TV on.

Think about your current morning and evening routines. If you were to be intentional about them, what would you change? Make a list. Which of these changes could you easily implement tomorrow? I invite you to try to make just one of them tomorrow and see how it impacts your day.

When I took a moment to pause and look at my routines, I made a number of changes. The first thing I did was buy an alarm clock. I realized that the mere act of picking up my phone to turn off the alarm created too many temptations to engage with the world (news, work, social media) before I was ready.

The second thing I did was a practice a meditation teacher shared with me years ago—a daily check-in. This means checking in with yourself about how you're doing. I say to myself, as soon as I wake up, "Good morning, Zee; how are you doing?" I use my name because it creates a feeling of being cared for. It's personal and it feels warm and loving. I take a quick moment to answer myself. If I'm cranky, I say "Cranky." The simple acknowledgment of this feeling gives me the opportunity to do something about it, either to ask myself why, or to nurture myself with something to make me feel better. If I'm feeling energetic and ready . . . well, that sets the tone for the whole day!

I invite you to try this right now. Ask yourself how you are doing. What's your answer? Now try this tomorrow morning when you wake up. See what your answer is then and how it's changed.

In addition to my daily check-in, I started meditating for a few minutes every morning as well. At first I started out with five minutes so that I couldn't come up with excuses about not having time. I wanted it to be easy and doable. After this became a regular practice, I started gradually increasing the amount of time. Some people aren't into meditation and choose to just spend some quiet time reflecting. Others use this time for prayer. Regardless of what you choose to do, there is something powerful about pausing and taking a few minutes for yourself before getting caught up in the hustle and bustle of the day.

After adding meditation to my routine, I started journaling for a few minutes every day, writing down whatever was on my mind. If there are difficult, emotional things, this practice gives them a space to be heard so that they won't be as distracting during the rest of the day. Sometimes my morning journaling morphs into my to-do list, which helps me get organized. Sometimes it includes a list of things that I'm grateful for. There is no set agenda for this practice, because it is a space for your thoughts to be expressed. Some say that this practice allows you to be more creative during your day, because getting these thoughts out clears space for the creativity to flow!

I also like to set an intention for the day. Sometimes it might focus on something I'm working on personally, like having more patience, being more present during meetings, or being open to trying new things. Other times it's about something I need, like taking some time for myself or taking deep breaths when times get tough. Why set intentions? The most obvious reason is that it increases the likelihood of it happening! The more scientific explanation is that the region in our brain called the reticular activating system filters out any unnecessary information so that only the important things get through. By deciding what's important to you upfront, your brain is then programmed to focus on those areas.

The last thing I experimented with in my morning routine was exercise. It's no secret that exercise increases endorphins, gives you more energy, and is generally good for your health. The reason I say I experimented is that time was the biggest barrier here. You might have read my new morning routine and thought, *Well, how does she have time for all that? I need sleep! That doesn't work for me!* In fact, up until the exercise experiment, everything I do takes no more than fifteen minutes. My daily check-in takes a few seconds, followed by five minutes of meditating and five minutes of journaling, and setting an intention could take a few seconds or a few minutes. Fifteen minutes that could change the entire trajectory of your day!

However, depending on what you do for exercise, it could add a good chunk of time. So, for me, on the days that I have time and can easily swing it, I work out. On the days that I don't have time, I do something really short, such as a ten-minute online-yoga routine, or playing one of my favorite songs and dancing for a bit. Just moving my body to the music for a three-minute song gets my blood flowing! I invite you to try it one morning! If you are self-conscious about people you live with judging you, just grab some headphones, go to a private place (the bathroom, the basement, etc.), and let your body move freely. Dance like no one's watching!

For my evening routines, I started being intentional about going to bed at the same time. I leave my phone outside of my bedroom. I limit electronic devices for the final hour before I go to sleep. During that hour, I light some incense or a candle. Aromatherapy has so many benefits, including reducing stress, anxiety, and pain, as well as improving sleep quality.

Intentional Morning & Evening Routines

Morning

- ✓ Daily check-in
- ✓ Set an intention
- ✓ Drink water
- ✓ Delay picking up your phone

Either Morning or Evening

- ✓ Exercise
- ✓ Gratitude list
- ✓ Journal
- ✓ Meditate
- ✓ Aromatherapy

Either Morning or Evening

- ✓ Sleep at the same time
- ✓ Phone on Do Not Disturb
- ✓ Do one thing that you love
- ✓ Read a book
- ✓ Family ritual
- ✓ Plan for tomorrow

During that hour, I make a gratitude list. Note that some people like to do this in the morning; both are equally effective. I write down three things I'm grateful for. You can try this right now. What are you grateful for in this moment? What are the first things that come to mind? They can be really simple, even one word. Sometimes my three things are my family, the sun, and love. Sometimes the three things end up being the same as yesterday's, and that's okay, too! I have friends who take this a step further and create a family ritual of gratitude that they do with their children every evening. Research shows that the practice of gratitude has a number of benefits, from opening the door to more relationships, to improving physical and psychological health, to improving our sleep quality and boosting our self-esteem!

Before I go to bed, I make sure to do one thing that I love. Sometimes that is reading a book. Other times it's taking a bath. Regardless, it's something that brings me joy.

On the opposite page are some suggested best practices to optimize your morning and evening routines.

Self-Care Practice 2: Treat Yo'self Weekly

As a Black woman, I have found myself constantly focused on making sure everyone else was taken care of. Whether it's at work or at home, it is what others have expected of me, and, honestly, what I have expected of myself, especially when I look at the model that my elders set for me. My grandmother cleaned other people's homes and took care of their children, on top of taking care of her own! But what did she do for herself? I can't help but think of Janet Jackson's song "What Have You Done for Me Lately," except that I like to reframe it as "What have you done for *you* lately?" When was the last time you treated yourself? When was the last time you did something just for you? You know you deserve it, so why not?

I invite you to think about ways to treat yourself every week. It can be something very small, like going for a walk or eating a piece of chocolate. It could be taking the time to draw a bath with Epsom salts and some lavender essential oil. Even taking a few minutes to massage your temples can have a huge impact on your day. Maybe you need some time with your friends, and you ask your partner to watch the kids for the evening. I have a friend who, every three months, gets a hotel room nearby for a weekend, a spa treatment, and her favorite novel, and indulges in "me time."

If you are having trouble coming up with what your "treat yo'self" practices might be, consider finishing this sentence:

I feel restored when . . .

When do you feel restored? Do that!

It's easy to make excuses for why we can't do these things, whether it's time, or money, or responsibilities. I encourage you to stay away from this dirty word of *can't* and think about what you *can* do! Put it on your calendar. Even a small thing, every week. Hold yourself accountable for showing yourself some love! You are worth it. You deserve it.

Key Points to Remember

- Regardless of what happens, the most important thing to remember throughout all of it is self-care and self-love. We can't control what other people do or say, but we can control all that is within.

- To truly love ourselves, we must take care of ourselves.

- Take the time to identify what you need to feel whole. Consider how you would finish this sentence: "I feel restored when . . ."

Mindfulness Practice Toolkit

Mindfulness Practice 31: What Do I Love about Myself?

When you are exhausted and daily challenges start to impact your self-esteem and your sense of self:

1 Find a quiet place and get your journal or another option for recording your thoughts.

2 Take a deep breath.

3 Set a timer for five minutes.

4 Write your answer to the question, "What do I love about myself?"

   a Write the first things that come to mind. Don't think too hard about it. If you can't come up with anything, just start writing anyway, even if it's to write "I have no idea what I love about myself."

   b If you feel really stuck, think about what someone who loves you would say, and consider whether you agree with them. If so, write it down!

5 When the five minutes are up, take a moment to read what you wrote.

6 Close your eyes and experience what it feels like to know and appreciate all the amazing things that are a part of you!

Mindfulness Practice 32: Intentional Morning and Evening Routines

To maintain a solid foundation for mental and physical health, so that you can handle any and all challenges that come your way:

1 Think about your typical mornings and evenings today. Write down what happens from the moment you wake up until you roll into your day. Write down what your evenings look like in the few hours before you go to sleep.

2 If you were to be intentional about your morning and evening routines, what would you change? For some ideas, reference the suggested best practices on page 199.

3 Choose one of the potential changes you identified that you could implement tomorrow.

4 Tomorrow, implement just that one thing and see how it feels.

5 Commit to additional changes that you think are feasible and incorporate them in your everyday life.

Mindfulness Practice 33: Treat Yo'self Weekly

If you want to prioritize self-care so that your mind and body can handle any and all challenges that come your way:

1 Think about what you can do on a weekly basis to treat yourself.

2 If you have difficulty coming up with ideas, take five minutes to finish this sentence in your journal: "I feel restored when . . ."

3 Once you have identified things you can do, commit to doing at least one thing every week. Put it on your calendar, and hold yourself accountable for showing yourself some love! You are worth it. You deserve it.

CHAPTER TWELVE

Mindfulness and Breathwork Toolkit

Just as you might take ibuprofen for headaches or antihistamines for allergies, you can use specific mindfulness and breathwork tools based on how you're feeling and what you're going through. Below is your guide to the thirty-four practices shared in this book. I encourage you to revisit these practices whenever you need them. You deserve to feel good, so why not take it into your own hands and make it happen, regardless of the challenges that come your way?

Video tutorials of key practices can be found at zeeclarke.com/resources to guide you on your journey of self-care.

Anxiety and Insomnia

4-7-8 Breathing (pg 125) When you are experiencing anxiety, whether it is due to the intense pressure to be flawless in your performance or endless worries about negative events that might happen because of your race or gender.

Humming Bee Breath (pg 52) To calm you down when you are having trouble sleeping or your mind is spiraling. *Note that the Humming Bee Breath can also be helpful for improving concentration if you are about to embark on a critical project.*

Overwhelmed and Needing Some Grounding

Name the Emotion (pg 70) When you are experiencing intense emotions, and the feelings are overwhelming.

Three-Part Breath (pg 14) When you want to feel more grounded.

Hand to Heart (pg 36) When you're triggered by something awful, such as witnessing the assault on Black lives, and you need to self-soothe.

Alternate-Nostril Breathing* (pg 148) Before walking into a meeting that you know will be stressful or triggering.

Visualization: A World Where You Are Safe, Valued, and Loved (pg 53) When you are feeling overwhelmed and perhaps disheartened by how unsafe this world can be.

Witnessing the Suffering of Others

Sending and Receiving (a.k.a. *Tonglen*) (pg 36) When others are suffering, and you want to send them love and support.

Triggered by the Police, Microaggressions +: In the Moment

Belly Breath (pg 70) When you are triggered in the moment, whether it's police harassment or an offensive comment, and you need to calm your nervous system.

---

* Alternate-Nostril Breathing Is inspired by the traditional *Nadi Shodhana pranayama*. It should not be practiced while suffering from a cold, the flu, or a fever.

Extra-Long Exhalation (pg 88) When someone says something offensive and irritating, and you want to respond from a calmer place.

Triggered by the Police, Microaggressions +: After the Incident

RAIN Meditation (pg 71) To heal after you have experienced a microaggression or traumatic event.

Anger

Cooling Breath (pg 105) When your blood is boiling and you are so angry at what you have just experienced.

Breath of Fire (pg 149) When you are feeling really angry about something that was said or done and you need to release it.

Enhanced Breath of Fire (pg 150) When the anger is extremely intense and all-consuming and you need a little extra push to release it.

Tension Release

Neck Roll (pg 37) When you've just experienced something very emotionally charged and need to release tension from your body.

Conscious Dance Release (pg 151) When you've had a hard day and you feel like you just can't handle any more.

Exhaustion

Bellows Breath (pg 126) When you are feeling exhausted and you need a boost of energy to get you through the day.

Frustration around Not Being Seen or Heard

Straw Breathing (pg 53) When you get really frustrated because you don't feel heard, at the doctor's office or elsewhere.

Squeeze and Release (pg 149) When you are annoyed and frustrated because you feel like you're not being seen.

The Only

"I Get To . . . " (pg 127) When you find yourself frustrated or uncomfortable because of the challenges that come with being "the only."

Boundary Setting

The Power of No (pg 126) When you are being asked to do things that make you uncomfortable or are more than you have the bandwidth for.

Today, I Choose Me (pg 104) If you're debating whether you should set boundaries with others, prioritizing their comfort over your own.

Imposter Syndrome and Boosting Self-Confidence

When you experience imposter syndrome, remember the acronym WEBAV:

Welcoming the Voice
Evidence Gathering
Breathwork
Affirmations
Visualization

Welcoming the Voice (pg 172) When you hear your imposter-syndrome voice start making negative commentary in your head.

Evidence Gathering (pg 173) To address negative self-talk and the statements your imposter-syndrome voice says about you.

Solar Plexus Breath (pg 173) When your imposter-syndrome voice is so distracting that you need some grounding.

Lion's Breath (pg 105) When you need to build confidence to allow your true voice to shine, whether it's making a big presentation at work, correcting someone about your name, or forcing others to really see you.

Affirmations (pg 174) When you could use a reminder of how amazing you really are and when your brain could use some rewiring to get rid of negative thought patterns.

Visualization (pg 175) When there is a specific event or situation that you would like to do well in.

Deciding Whether to Code-Switch

Byron Katie's "The Work": Four Questions (pg 191) To address any limiting beliefs you might have and to help assess whether to code-switch.

What Do I Love about Myself? (pg 202) When code-switching is starting to impact your self-esteem and your sense of self.

Negativity around Blackness

Hear-Centered: What Does Being Black Mean to You? (pg 89) When all the negativity about stereotypes of Black people start to wear you down, and you could use a reminder of your personal truth.

Black People You Admire Most (pg 89) When you need a reminder about how amazing Black people really are.

Self-Care

Intentional Morning and Evening Routines (pg 203) To maintain a solid foundation for mental and physical health, so that you can handle any and all challenges that come your way.

Treat Yo'self Weekly (pg 203) To prioritize self-care and demonstrate through action just how much you love and value you!

Resources

Autonomic Dysfunction and POTS Center. "Overactive Sympathetic Nervous System." December 11, 2020. https://franklincardiovascular .com/overactive-sympathetic-nervous-system/.

Brach, Tara. *Radical Compassion: Learning to Love Yourself and Your World with the Practice of RAIN*. New York, NY: Penguin Life, 2019.

Brennan, Dan. "What Is Breath of Fire Yoga?," WebMD, November 27, 2021. https://www.webmd.com/balance/what-is-breath-of-fire-yoga.

Center for Substance Abuse Treatment. "Understanding the Impact of Trauma." In *Trauma-Informed Care in Behavioral Health Services*. Rockville, MD: Substance Abuse and Mental Health Services Administration, 2014.

Clance, Pauline R., and Suzanne Ament Imes. "The Imposter Phenomenon in High Achieving Women: Dynamics and Therapeutic Intervention." *Psychotherapy: Theory, Research & Practice* 15, no. 3 (1978): 241–47. https://doi.org/10.1037/h0086006.

Clark, Timothy R. *The 4 Stages of Psychological Safety: Defining the Path to Inclusion and Innovation*. Oakland, CA: Berrett-Koehler Publishers, 2020.

Dreisoerner, Aljoscha, Nina M. Junker, Wolff Schlotz, Julia Heimrich, Svenja Bloemeke, Beate Ditzen, and Rolf van Dick. "Self-Soothing Touch and Being Hugged Reduce Cortisol Responses to Stress: A Randomized Controlled Trial on Stress, Physical Touch, and Social Identity." *Comprehensive Psychoneuroendocrinology* 8 (2021): 100091. https://doi.org/10.1016/j.cpnec.2021.100091.

Edwards, Frank, Hedwig Lee, and Michael Esposito. "Risk of Being Killed by Police Use of Force in the United States by Age, Race–Ethnicity, and Sex." *Proceedings of the National Academy of Sciences* 116, no. 34 (2019): 16793–98. https://doi.org/10.1073/pnas.1821204116,

Fletcher, Jenna. "How to Use 4-7-8 Breathing for Anxiety." Medical News Today, February 12, 2019. https://www.medicalnewstoday.com/articles/324417.

Francis, Megan M. "Ida B. Wells and the Economics of Racial Violence." Items: Social Research Council, January 24, 2017. https://items.ssrc.org/reading-racial-conflict/ida-b-wells-and-the-economics-of-racial-violence/.

Germain, Atahabih. "11-Year-Old Black Boy Offered Gift Card in Response to Being Falsely Accused of Stealing at California Safeway." Atlanta Black Star. May 9, 2021. https://atlantablackstar.com/2021/05/09/11-year-old-black-boy-offered-gift-card-in-response-to-being-falsely-accused-of-stealing-at-california-safeway/.

Hoffman, Kelly M., Sophie Trawalter, Jordan R. Axt, and M. Norman Oliver. "Racial Bias in Pain Assessment and Treatment Recommendations, and False Beliefs about Biological Differences Between Blacks and Whites," Proceedings of the National Academy of Sciences 113, no. 16 (2016): 4296–301. https://doi.org/10.1073/pnas.1516047113.

Iati, Marisa, Jennifer Jenkins, and Sommer Brugal. "Nearly 250 Women Have Been Fatally Shot by Police since 2015." The Washington Post, September 4, 2020. https://www.washingtonpost.com/graphics/2020/investigations/police-shootings-women/.

Kang, Sonia K., Adam D. Galinsky, Laura J. Kray, and Aiwa Shirako. "Power Affects Performance When the Pressure Is On: Evidence for Low-Power Threat and High-Power Lift." Personality and Social Psychology Bulletin 41, no. 5 (2015): 726–35. https://doi.org/10.1177/0146167215577365.

Kross, Ethan, Emma Bruehlman-Senecal, Jiyoung Park, Aleah Burson, Adrienne Dougherty, Holly Shablack, Ryan Bremner, Jason Moser, and Ozlem Ayduk. "Self-Talk as a Regulatory Mechanism: How You Do It Matters." Journal of Personality and Social Psychology 106, no. 2 (2014): 304. https://doi.org/10.1037/a0035173.

Kuppusamy, Maheshkumar, Dilara Kamaldeen, Ravishankar Pitani, Julius Amaldas, and Poonguzhali Shanmugam. "Effects of Bhramari Pranayama on Health–A Systematic Review." *Journal of Traditional and Complementary Medicine* 8, no. 1 (2018): 11–16. https://doi.org/10.1016/j.jtcme.2017.02.003.

Lean In. "The State of Black Women in Corporate America." Accessed March 7, 2022. https://leanin.org/research/state-of-black-women-in-corporate-america/introduction.

Leonard, Jayne. "What Does Anxiety Feel Like and How Does It Affect the Body?," July 18, 2018. https://www.medicalnewstoday.com/articles/322510.

Lloyd, Camille. "Black Adults Disproportionately Experience Microaggressions." Gallup, July 15, 2020. https://news.gallup.com/poll/315695/black-adults-disproportionately-experience-microaggressions.aspx.

Logan, Trevan. "A Brief History of Black Names, from Perlie to Latasha." The Conversation, January 23, 2020. https://theconversation.com/a-brief-history-of-black-names-from-perlie-to-latasha-130102.

Maese, Rick. "For Olympians, Seeing (in Their Minds) Is Believing (It Can Happen)." *The Washington Post*, July 28, 2016. https://www.washingtonpost.com/sports/olympics/for-olympians-seeing-in-their-minds-is-believing-it-can-happen/2016/07/28/6966709c-532e-11e6-bbf5-957ad17b4385_story.html.

McCluney, Courtney L., Kathrina Robotham, Serenity Lee, Richard Smith, and Myles Durkee. "The Costs of Code-Switching." *Harvard Business Review*, November 15, 2019. https://hbr.org/2019/11/the-costs-of-codeswitching.

Miller, Stephen. "Black Workers Still Earn Less Than Their White Counterparts." Society for Human Resources Management, June 11, 2020. https://www.shrm.org/resourcesandtools/hr-topics/compensation/pages/racial-wage-gaps-persistence-poses-challenge.aspx.

Monteiro, Nicole M., and Diana J. Wall. "African Dance as Healing Modality throughout the Diaspora: The Use of Ritual and Movement to Work through Trauma." *The Journal of Pan African Studies* 4, no. 6 (2011): 234–52.

Morin. Amy. "7 Scientifically Proven Benefits of Gratitude That Will Motivate You to Give Thanks Year-Round." *Forbes*, November 23, 2014. https://www.forbes.com/sites/amymorin/2014/11/23/7-scientifically-proven-benefits-of-gratitude-that-will-motivate-you-to-give-thanks-year-round/?sh=48ff765183c0.

Pazzanese, Christina. "How Unjust Police Killings Damage the Mental Health of Black Americans." *Harvard Gazette*, May 13, 2021. https://news.harvard.edu/gazette/story/2021/05/how-unjust-police-killings-damage-the-mental-health-of-black-americans/.

Pazzanese, Christina. "Key to Doing Your Best at Work? Be Yourself." *Harvard Gazette*, March 10, 2021. https://hbswk.hbs.edu/item/key-to-doing-your-best-at-work-be-yourself.

Pramanik, T., B. Pudasaini, and R. Prajapati. "Immediate Effect of a Slow Pace Breathing Exercise Bhramari Pranayama on Blood Pressure and Heart Rate." *Nepal Medical College Journal* 12, no. 3 (2010): 154–57.

Richards, Carl. "Learning to Deal with the Impostor Syndrome." *The New York Times*, October 26, 2015. https://www.nytimes.com/2015/10/26/your-money/learning-to-deal-with-the-impostor-syndrome.html.

Rodriguez, Tori. "Descendants of Holocaust Survivors Have Altered Stress Hormones." *Scientific American Mind*, March 1, 2015. https://www.scientificamerican.com/article/descendants-of-holocaust-survivors-have-altered-stress-hormones/.

Sahadi, Jeanne. "After Years of Talking about Diversity, the Number of Black Leaders at US Companies Is Still Dismal." *CNN Business*, June 29, 2020. https://edition.cnn.com/2020/06/02/success/diversity-and-black-leadership-in-corporate-america/index.html.

Sesko, Amanda K., and Monica Biernat. "Prototypes of Race and Gender: The Invisibility of Black Women." *Journal of Experimental Social Psychology* 46, no. 2 (2010): 356–60. https://doi.org/10.1016/j.jesp.2009.10.016.

Sharma, Vivek Kumar, Madanmohan Trakroo, Velkumary Subramaniam, M. Rajajeyakumar, Anand B. Bhavanani, and Ajit Sahai. "Effect of Fast and Slow Pranayama on Perceived Stress and Cardiovascular Parameters in Young Health-Care Students." *International Journal of Yoga* 6, no. 2 (2013): 104.

Smith, Alexis Nicole, Marla Baskerville Watkins, Jamie J. Ladge, and Pamela Carlton. "Making the Invisible Visible: Paradoxical Effects of Intersectional Invisibility on the Career Experiences of Executive Black Women." *Academy of Management Journal* 62, no. 6 (2019): 1705–34. https://doi.org/10.5465/amj.2017.1513.

Swetlitz, Ike, "Some Medical Students Still Think Black Patients Feel Less Pain Than Whites." Stat. April 4, 2016. https://www.statnews.com/2016/04/04/medical-students-beliefs-race-pain/.

Trivedi, Madhukar H., "The Link between Depression and Physical Symptoms." *Primary Care Companion to the Journal of Clinical Psychiatry* 6, suppl 1 (2004): 12–16.

Torino, G. "How Racism and Microaggressions Lead to Worse Health." *Center for Health Journalism*, November 10, 2017. https://centerforhealthjournalism.org/2017/11/08/how-racism-and-microaggressuions-lead-worse-health.

Watson, Stephanie, and Kristeen Cherney. "The Effects of Sleep Deprivation on Your Body." Healthline, December 15, 2021. https://www.healthline.com/health/sleep-deprivation/effects-on-body.

The Work, 2022. https://thework.com/.

Acknowledgments

First, I want to acknowledge every individual who can relate to at least one of the experiences I described in this book. You help me to feel in my bones that I am not alone.

To the trailblazers, those who came first and paved the way for us, I inhale with gratitude!

To my ancestors, especially my great-grandmother Maria Abail, for being present and offering guidance throughout it all.

To my parents, for doing their best to give me the tools I needed to survive in this world.

To my brothers, Ernesto and Raphael, for teaching me that we must each forge our own unique path.

Joy Limpuangthip: Thank you for showing me the light, and for sharing what you have learned on your journey, which helped get me through the hardest of times.

Thembi Ford: You have always been my inspiration. Thank you for sharing your stories around race in a way that helped me find humor despite the pain. Thank you for being you.

Julian Breece: Thank you for encouraging me to get into meditation in the first place. Thank you for reminding me where I'm from, where I'm going, and what I'm capable of.

Kriste Peoples: Thank you for being on the ground with me to help our sisters heal, in Denver and across the country. Black and Brown Women's Alliance helped me heal even as we helped others. Thank you for your honest and objective feedback on this book and all things.

Rianna Stefanakis and Joanne Lee: Thank you for letting me cry on your shoulders throughout the many years of trials and tribulations. And thank you for helping me dance the pain away.

Jasmine Wiley (a.k.a. Narkita): Thank you for shining a spotlight on our voices, and for teaching me that art can be a powerful tool in social justice movements and driving change. Thank you for being my soul sister.

Ezekiel Nance: Thank you for digging deep into your own experiences, for the open-hearted discussions around the meanings behind them, and for being an amazing sounding board during the writing process.

Sahara Clement: Your feedback was game changing. Empathetic, strategic, heart-felt, actionable. Everything I could have ever wanted in an editor. I'm excited to see all the magic that you bring into this world.

Jess Regel: Thank you for seeing an unpolished stone and knowing how to transform it into a gem. Thank you for believing in me.

Saira Rao: Thank you for planting the seed that made this book a reality.

Kim Keating: Thank you for taking in a seventeen-year-old and showing me what the world was like. Thank you for being my mentor and friend.

Muriel Wilkins: Thank you for helping me find the courage that was buried within. Thank you for keeping me on track in moments of overwhelm. I appreciate you more than you know.

To the amazing sisters of the Black Women's Professional Community Dinner hosted by Facebook, these quarterly gatherings were a godsend during my tech career in Silicon Valley. Thank you for being real about your experiences and for breaking bread (and Jamaican deliciousness) with me.

Special shout-out to LEAD and INROADS, which were instrumental in the early days of my career, and programs like MLT and SEO that have helped so many of my Black friends and colleagues.

Lastly, I would like to thank every program out there that is specifically focused on helping our people be the best that we can be, mentally, emotionally, and physically. We need you.

Ten Speed Press and the Ten Speed Press colophon are
registered trademarks of Penguin Random House LLC.

Typefaces: David Jonathan Ross' Roslindale, Klim's
Tiempos, Commercial Type's Graphik, and Kimberly
Geswein's Nothing You Could Do and Nothing You
Could Say

Library of Congress Cataloging-in-Publication Data is
on file with the publisher.

Hardcover ISBN: 978-1-9848-6099-6
eBook ISBN: 978-1-9848-6100-9

Printed in China

Editor: Sahara Clement | Production editor:
    Serena Wang
Designer: Isabelle Gioffredi | Art director: Kelly Booth
    | Production Designers: Mari Gill and Faith Hague
Production manager: Dan Myers
Copy editor: Jane Hardick
Publicist: Felix Cruz | Marketer: Brianne Sperber

10 9 8 7 6 5 4 3 2 1

First Edition